RELIGIONS TO inSPiRE

for KS3

Judaism

Lorraine Abbott

Series editor: Steve Clarke

DYNAMIC LEARNING

HODDER EDUCATION
AN HACHETTE UK COMPANY

For Ellie, Lucy and Holly

The Author and Publishers would like to thank Sara Leviten of The Board of Deputies of British Jews for advising them on the content of this book and Simon Goulden of the United Synagogue for advising them on the cover and general helpfulness.

The Author would like to thank the Latte Club who never cease in encouragement and caffeine provision! Also Megan and Nicole who are a source of inspiration as they continue to reinvent themselves and strive for better things; and Jess, Bertie, Kriesha, Clare, Alice and Emily – all of whom offer questioning and discussion that is sharp and perceptive.

The Publishers would like to thank the following for permission to reproduce copyright material:

Photo credits

t= top   b=bottom   c=centre   l=left   r=right

p. 4 tl © Philippe Lissac/Godong/Corbis, tr © Flirt/SuperStock, bl © Hanan Isachar/SuperStock, br © Ambient Images Inc./SuperStock; **p. 6** © Anyka – Fotolia; **p. 7** l © www.BibleLandPictures.com/Alamy, r © Pascal Deloche/Godong/Corbis; **p. 9** tl © Tim Page/Corbis, tr © Abba Richman – Fotolia, bl © Sean Gallup/Getty Images, br © Henry A. Barrios/ZUMA Press/Corbis; **pp. 10–11** © Hanan Isachar/Corbis; **p. 12** © herreneck – Fotolia; **p. 14** © ASAP/Alamy; **p. 15** © Noam – Fotolia; **p. 16** © Photodisc/Getty Images; **p. 18** © 2006 David Silverman/Getty Images; **p. 19** t © London Beth Din, bl Courtesy of STAR-K Kosher certification, br © Orthodox Union; **p. 22** © Graham Photography – Fotolia; **p. 24** © Photodisc/Getty Images; **p. 25** © 2007 PAL PILLAI/AFP/Getty Images; **pp. 28–29** © Pascal Deloche/Godong/Corbis; **p. 33** © Richard McBee; **p. 34** © Ms Add 11639 Abraham sacrificing Isaac, Pentateuchs, written in Hebrew (vellum), French School, (13th century)/British Library, London, UK Topham Picturepoint/The Bridgeman Art Library; **p. 35** © HAZEM BADER/AFP/Getty Images; **pp. 36–37** © Joshua Haviv – Fotolia; **pp. 38–39** © Ella – Fotolia; **p. 41** tl © paul prescott – Fotolia, tr Jim West/Alamy, c © Iwan Baan, b © Nir Alon/Demotix/Corbis; **p. 44** © Scott Speakes/Corbis; **p. 45** © Steve Clarke; **pp. 48–49** © Jeff Greenberg/Alamy; **p. 51** © Ruby/Alamy; **p. 55** © Hanan Isachar/Corbis; **p. 57** © Golden Pixels/SuperFusion/SuperStock; **p. 60** © Imagno/Getty Images; **p. 61** © DiMaggio/Kalish/Corbis; **p. 64** © JAMES STEVENSON/ SCIENCE PHOTO LIBRARY; **p. 66** © Godong/ Robert Harding World Imagery/Getty Images; **pp . 68–69** © Imagestate Media Partners Limited - Impact Photos/Alamy

Acknowledgements

All quotes from *The Holy Bible, New International Version Anglicised*, copyright © 1979, 1984 by Biblica, Inc. First Published in Great Britain in 1979 by Hodder & Stoughton Publishers, a division of Hachette UK Ltd.

Every effort has been made to trace all copyright holders, but if any have been inadvertently overlooked the Publishers will be pleased to make the necessary arrangements at the first opportunity.

Although every effort has been made to ensure that website addresses are correct at time of going to press, Hodder Education cannot be held responsible for the content of any website mentioned in this book. It is sometimes possible to find a relocated web page by typing in the address of the home page for a website in the URL window of your browser.

Hachette UK's policy is to use papers that are natural, renewable and recyclable products and made from wood grown in sustainable forests. The logging and manufacturing processes are expected to conform to the environmental regulations of the country of origin.

Orders: please contact Bookpoint Ltd, 130 Milton Park, Abingdon, Oxon OX14 4SB. Telephone: (44) 01235 827720. Fax: (44) 01235 400454. Lines are open 9.00–5.00, Monday to Saturday, with a 24-hour message answering service. Visit our website at www.hoddereducation.co.uk

© Lorraine Abbott 2012
First published in 2012 by
Hodder Education
An Hachette UK Company
Carmelite House, 50 Victoria Embankment
London EC4Y 0DZ

Impression number   5
Year   2016   2015

Cover photo © iStockphoto/Ionescu Bogdan Cristian
Illustrations by Barking Dog Art, Peter Lubach, Oxford Designers & Illustrators Ltd, Tony Kandell
Typeset in Minion regular 12.5pt/15pt by Wooden Ark
Printed in Dubai

A catalogue record for this title is available from the British Library

ISBN: 978 1444 12224 4

Contents

1.1 Who are the Jews?

There are approximately 15 million Jews worldwide.

King David established **Jerusalem** as the capital of Israel, with the Jewish temple at the centre.

In the UK today there are about 300,000 Jews.

Secular Jews are people who are Jewish by birth but who choose not to follow the religion.

A person is Jewish because they are born Jewish.

As you can see from the map on page 5, most Jews live in Israel.

The religion goes back 4000 years and was founded by **Abraham**.

Not all Jews are the same – they believe and practise their religion in different ways. The two main types of Jew are Orthodox and Progressive.

Israel is the land that the Jews believe was promised to them by God.

The symbol of Judaism is the **Star of David**.

Jews who choose to live very strict lives and follow their religious rules as closely as possible are known as **Orthodox Jews**.

Progressive Jews believe that their religion needs to move with the times and that some religious practices need to be reformed in order to fit in with the modern world.

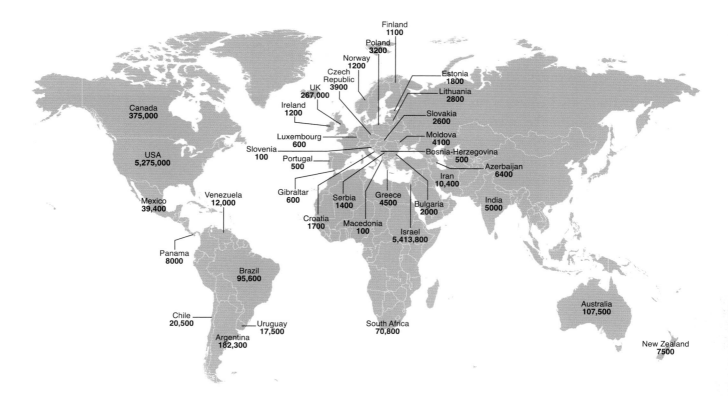

Finland
1100

Poland
3200

Norway
1200

Czech
Republic
3900

UK
267,000

Ireland
1200

Estonia
1800

Lithuania
2800

Slovakia
2600

Luxembourg
600

Moldova
4100

Slovenia
100

Bosnia-Herzegovina
500

Portugal
500

Azerbaijan
6400

Gibraltar
600

Iran
10,400

Serbia
1400

Greece
4500

India
5000

Croatia
1700

Bulgaria
2000

Macedonia
100

Israel
5,413,800

Canada
375,000

USA
5,275,000

Mexico
39,400

Venezuela
12,000

Panama
8000

Brazil
95,600

Chile
20,500

Uruguay
17,500

Argentina
182,300

South Africa
70,800

Australia
107,500

New Zealand
7500

The larger map above shows that the highest number of Jews can be found in Israel. The state of Israel was established in 1948 after the Second World War. The Jews originally came from the Middle East. The smaller map on the left shows the Middle East today; see pages 62–63 for further discussion.

Knowledge check

1 What is the worldwide population of Jews?

2 Where in the world do most Jews live?

3 Who is the founder of Judaism?

4 What makes a person Jewish?

5 What are the two main types of Judaism?

6 What is the difference between the two main Jewish groups?

Just like Islam and Christianity, Judaism is a **monotheistic** religion. This means that all Jews believe that there is only one God. Abraham is the founder of Judaism because he made his tribe worship this one God.

The Holy Book of the Jews is the **Torah**. In the Torah, God makes a **covenant** with Abraham. Through this covenant God promises Abraham and his people a land of their own and many descendants. Abraham has to obey God's commands. It is because of their special relationship with God that the Jews seek to obey him. One of the most important laws is to love God. This is seen in the most important prayer in Judaism called the **Shema**.

God led Abraham and his people into the land of Canaan, now known as Israel, and through many battles with other tribes the Jews took this land as God had promised. Even today there are battles over who the land of Israel belongs to.

This is a **mezuzah**. A mezuzah is a small box that contains a scroll with the words of the Shema written on it. The mezuzah is fixed onto the right-hand doorpost of each door in a Jewish home, except the bathroom and the toilet.

'Hear, O Israel: The Lord is our God, the Lord is one. You shall love the Lord your God with all your heart, with all your soul and with all your might.'

The Shema is written in Hebrew in the mezuzah. Here, we have translated the opening lines.

Activity A

Produce a mock interview with a Jewish person.

1 Think about the things people might want to know about Judaism, and write them out as questions to be asked by the interviewer.

2 Then use the information from this chapter and other sources (for example, the Internet) to answer the questions from a Jewish perspective.

3 You could either complete this task as a written script or produce a recording of the interview.

Activity B

The Jews have many rules from God that they aim to keep out of love for him. Their most important act of obedience is to love God. This is seen in the words at the start of the Shema.

1 Design a questionnaire to find out what school rules people think are the most important.

2 Get people to complete your questionnaire and evaluate what you find out.

3 Then use the information from this chapter and other sources (for example, the Internet) to compare the rules in Judaism to school rules. What similarities and differences can you identify? Present your findings in two columns.

In the Shema (left), Jews are told to bind God's commands 'on your hand, and as ornaments between your eyes, and you shall write them on the doorposts of your house' (see below).

Activity C

Why do you think it is important for British people to learn about Judaism in the twenty-first century?

1 Use information from this chapter to help you, and write down your thoughts in the form of a spidergram.

2 Then turn it into a leaflet to advertise Judaism. Find photographs or draw pictures to add to your leaflet.

Activity D

1 Why do Jews tie the words of the Shema onto their foreheads and arms during worship and keep them nailed to their doorposts?

2 Do you think Jews should need to be reminded to love God? Give reasons for your answer.

1.2 What are the Jewish holy books?

Learning objectives

You will ...
- learn what the Jewish holy books are
- understand the importance of the Torah
- think about how and why Jews use the Torah.

The Jewish holy scriptures are known as the **Tenakh**. The Tenakh has three sections:

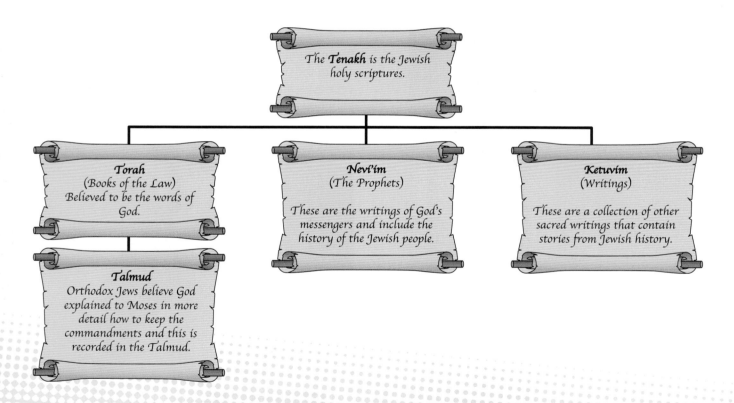

The **Tenakh** is the Jewish holy scriptures.

Torah
(Books of the Law)
Believed to be the words of God.

Talmud
Orthodox Jews believe God explained to Moses in more detail how to keep the commandments and this is recorded in the Talmud.

Nevi'im
(The Prophets)

These are the writings of God's messengers and include the history of the Jewish people.

Ketuvim
(Writings)

These are a collection of other sacred writings that contain stories from Jewish history.

Knowledge check

1 What is the Tenakh?

2 How many sections is the Tenakh divided into?

3 What are the main sections of the Tenakh called?

4 What is the link between the rules given in the Torah and the writings of the **Talmud**?

5 What does the Nevi'im contain?

6 What does the Ketuvim contain?

The importance of the Torah

Hebrew is the language of Judaism, and the word Torah comes from Hebrew. It means teachings. The Torah is the most important part of the Tenakh because it is believed to contain the words of God and it includes the rules about how Jews should live. The Torah scroll is always treated with the utmost respect by Jews.

A **yad** is used to follow the words when reading from the Torah. This protects the parchment from becoming dirty and damaged from being touched by hands.

To show respect for the Torah it is dressed when not in use. This protects the scrolls and shows respect for them. They have a cover called a **mantle**. Torahs are kept in a special cupboard called an **Ark** in the **synagogue**.

Every Torah scroll is without mistakes and is written by a **Sofer**. A Sofer is a Jewish scribe who handwrites the Torah.

The Torah is paraded around the synagogue before it is put away.

How and why Jews use the Torah

A portion of the Torah is read every week in the synagogue and particular pieces are read at festivals.

The Torah is carried from the Ark and around the synagogue to the **bimah** before it is read. The men may try to touch the mantle with the tassels of their **tallits** (prayer shawls).

As the Torah is carried past, the Jews will then kiss the tassels to show their love for the word of God.

Orthodox men wearing teffilin (the shema bound to their heads and arms) and tallits in a service at the synagogue.

All Jews believe the Torah contains the words of God and gives them advice from him on how to live.

The Torah is full of **mitzvot**. These are God-given commandments, and Jews aim to know and to follow these commands.

The Torah helps Jews to be aware of God's involvement with their history and how he has made a relationship with them.

The Torah reminds Jews of the special covenant God made with Abraham. It makes clear that they should only worship this one God.

During difficult times in their history faithful Jews have trusted in God's promises in the Torah and this has given them strength and hope. For example, Jews may look at the account in Exodus about how God rescued the Jews from slavery in Egypt.

The Torah includes rules about how to worship God. For example, in the book of Numbers a description is given about clothes, which is why Jews use tallits.

The word of God?

Orthodox Jews believe the Torah contains the exact words of God as they were first given to the Israelite leader, Moses. Other Jews, including Progressive Jews, think the Torah contains important advice from God about living but that the words are from inspired men of God several thousand years ago, not God's actual words.

Activity A

1 Make an information sheet to describe how the Jews treat the Torah.

2 On your sheet link how the Jews treat the Torah to how this demonstrates the respect and importance they have for it.

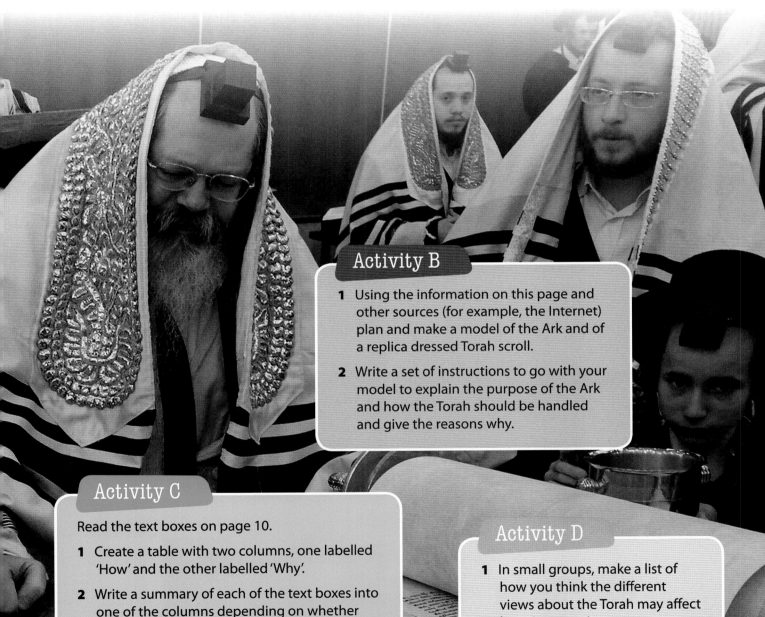

Activity B

1 Using the information on this page and other sources (for example, the Internet) plan and make a model of the Ark and of a replica dressed Torah scroll.

2 Write a set of instructions to go with your model to explain the purpose of the Ark and how the Torah should be handled and give the reasons why.

Activity C

Read the text boxes on page 10.

1 Create a table with two columns, one labelled 'How' and the other labelled 'Why'.

2 Write a summary of each of the text boxes into one of the columns depending on whether you think it gives an explanation of how the Torah is used or why Jews use the Torah.

Activity D

1 In small groups, make a list of how you think the different views about the Torah may affect how Jews use it.

2 Hold a class debate to decide whether it matters if the words of the Torah come directly from God or from humans.

1.3 How do Jews worship in the synagogue?

Learning objectives

You will ...
- identify the main features in the worship area of a synagogue
- compare the different ways in which Jews worship
- understand the importance of worship for Jews.

Jews believe that they have a personal relationship with God. The Torah tells them that God listens when they speak to him, that he knows what is on their minds and that he responds to their prayers.

Jews believe that there is no place they can go to escape the presence of God. Jews can and do pray privately and alone but most Jews will also make time to worship with other Jews in a synagogue. The word synagogue means gathering. The synagogue is the gathering, or meeting, place for Jews.

A weekly worship service is held in synagogues on the holy day of Shabbat. Shabbat lasts from sunset on Friday until sunset on Saturday. All synagogues have the same important features used during worship.

In the centre of the synagogue there is a raised platform called the bimah. The Torah is read from here.

In some synagogues, for example Orthodox ones, there is separate seating for the women and the men. This is so that they do not become distracted from worship by one another. However, in a Progressive synagogue men and women may sit together.

Above the Ark hangs a lamp called the **ner tamid**. It never goes out. This symbolises that God is always there.

On the wall facing Jerusalem is the Ark. It is the cupboard where the Torah is kept. This is the holiest part of the building. It is raised up to show how important the Torah is.

Fixed to the wall above or beside the Ark are the Ten Commandments that God gave to Moses. These are usually written in Hebrew.

Orthodox men try to attend prayers at the synagogue on a Friday evening and then they go home to celebrate Shabbat with their family. Progressive synagogues have later services so that the whole family can attend after they have had their Shabbat meal at home.

The order of service is in the Jewish prayer book, called the **siddur**. An Orthodox service is usually led by the **chazan**. The chazan chants prayers and reads sections of the Torah in Hebrew. His singing leads the congregation through worship. Some Progressive synagogues no longer have a chazan; instead the **rabbi** will read the service in English and musical instruments are used to lead the singing.

When the Torah is to be read in the synagogue the scroll is taken from the Ark and carried at shoulder height in a procession around the synagogue. The congregation stand and focus on the Torah. The Torah is read from the bimah either in Hebrew (Orthodox service) or in English (Progressive service). Often the reading is done by the rabbi. There is another procession back to the Ark when the scroll is being put away. This procession takes the longest route to involve the whole community.

Knowledge check

1 What type of relationship do Jews believe that they have with God?
2 Where do Jews believe that they can go to escape God's presence?
3 Where do Jews go to worship together?
4 What is the meaning of the word 'synagogue'?
5 What is Shabbat?

Activity A

1 Create a floorplan diagram of a synagogue using the photograph opposite to help you.
2 Label the floorplan and summarise the purpose or importance of each feature using bullet points below your labelled diagram.

Activity B

In small groups create a board game that takes the players through an act of worship at the synagogue. Use the information on this page as well as making use of other resources, for example, the Internet.

1 In your game allow players to make choices about whether they are going to follow an Orthodox service or a more Progressive service.
2 The winner will be the first player to complete every stage of worship.

Activity C

1 In pairs create a radio or TV discussion between an Orthodox Jew and a Progressive Jew.
2 In your programme you must include why worship is important to them and why they each believe that their form or worship is the right way.

Activity D

1 Identify what you think are the most important criteria for worship.
2 Give a reason for each of the criteria that you have identified.
3 Explain whether you think either Orthodox or Progressive worship best fits the criteria that you have identified.

1.4 How do Jews keep the Shabbat Mitzvot?

Learning objectives

You will ...
- identify how the Shabbat Mitzvot are kept
- understand why Shabbat is celebrated
- evaluate the importance to family life of coming together on a regular basis.

In the Torah Jews are told to keep one day a week aside as a holy day. In the fourth commandment, or **mitzvah** (plural mitzvot), God tells the Jews not to work on the **Sabbath**. They are to keep this one day holy, as a day of rest dedicated to God.

The Shabbat is kept as a special day to spend time with the family and to worship God. The Torah lists 39 jobs that cannot be done once Shabbat begins at Friday sunset. For example, Jews are commanded not to use a hammer, start a fire or bake on the Shabbat. All housework and preparations for Shabbat have to be completed before the sunset. Shabbat is then kept until Saturday sunset.

The father says a prayer over the two loaves of bread called **challah**. The challah is a reminder of God's care for the Jews. When the Jews escaped slavery in Egypt they went into the desert to hide. During this time God gave them bread to survive. The bread is eaten with a little salt. In the past salt was expensive and so this is a symbol to show the best is kept to celebrate on Shabbat.

The family gather together to eat the Shabbat meal. The father starts the meal by praying over a glass of red wine. Everyone has a sip.

Men may go to the synagogue to welcome the Shabbat in.

After the blessings the family eat a meal together.

Just before sunset, a Jewish wife or mother starts the Shabbat celebrations. She lights two candles and says a prayer called the **kiddush**.

At the end of the meal a special blessing is said.

In many Jewish homes, families may sing special Shabbat songs together or the father may tell the children stories from Jewish history.

As Shabbat ends the family smell some sweet special spices that are kept in a small wooden box. This is to symbolise the hope that the sweetness of Shabbat will last through the week.

To end Shabbat on Saturday sunset a prayer called the **Havdalah** is said as a plaited candle is lit. Havdalah means 'separation' and it marks the separation of Shabbat from the other days in the week.

Knowledge check

1 Why do Jews keep the Shabbat Mitzvot?
2 What does Shabbat give Jews time for?
3 How many precise jobs does the Torah forbid on Shabbat?
4 When does Shabbat begin?
5 When does Shabbat end?

Activity A

1 List the types of jobs Jews will need to do before the start of Shabbat. Use the photographs and text boxes on pages 14 and 15 to help you.

2 Explain why it is important to complete these tasks before Shabbat begins.

3 What benefits do you think there may be if all people set a day aside each week and avoided doing work on that one day?

Activity B

1 Read through the ways that Jews celebrate Shabbat described on pages 14 and 15.

2 Decide which order the pieces of information should go in so that they are arranged in time order.

3 Write a series of diary entries based on this information, recording a Jewish family's Shabbat celebrations.

What I like about Shabbat

I look forward to Shabbat because I get to spend time with my family.

We always chat about what has happened in the week and our plans for the coming week.

Dad is always home from work in time for Shabbat and I love listening to the amazing stories from our Jewish history.

This time each week helps me to feel secure and during the week I look forward to the space and the peace that Shabbat gives me.

Activity C

1 Imagine that you are a journalist for a newspaper. You want to find out how the regular celebration of Shabbat in Jewish families affects their relationships with each other. What questions might you ask? Think about how a Jewish family might answer them. Use the information on this page to help you.

2 Write a newspaper article about the effect of Shabbat on relationships within Jewish families. You could include your questions and the answers you think the Jewish family might have given you.

Activity D

1 In small groups discuss the strengths and weaknesses of a family setting aside one day a week to spend together and to focus on their religion.

2 Imagine that you are a government advisor on family life. Write a report recommending or advising against encouraging families to spend time together once a week, every week. Use examples from the Jewish practice of Shabbat and points from your small group discussion to support your recommendations.

1.5 Why do Jews keep kosher?

Learning objectives

You will ...
- learn what it means to keep kosher
- understand why Jews keep kosher.

The Torah clearly states what Jews should and should not eat. It also explains how they should kill animals to make sure the animal's death is as painless as possible. Keeping to the food laws laid down in the Torah is another example of how Jews keep the mitzvot. The food laws are known as the **kosher** rules. Kosher foods are those that Jews are allowed to eat.

A Jewish butcher must slaughter an animal using the kosher method, by cutting the animal's throat.

Any fish with fins and scales is allowed but shellfish and eels are not.

Basic Kosher Laws

Only meat from permitted animals can be eaten. Meat from pigs, for example bacon and pork, are non-kosher, whereas chicken is kosher.

Meat and dairy products cannot be eaten in the same meal.

Blood must be removed from all meat, because the life of the animal is contained in the blood.

- Orthodox Jews stick closely to these rules and may even have a divided kitchen. In such a kitchen there may be two sinks as well as one set of pans and cupboards with blue handles for use with dairy products and one set with red handles for meat products. This is to avoid mixing the two, which would break kosher rules.

- Progressive Jews vary in how closely they keep to kosher rules. For example, some may eat kosher food but not necessarily have a divided kitchen.

Knowledge check

1 What are the food laws in Judaism also known as?

2 Where do Jews get their food laws from?

3 Give one reason why Jews follow the kosher rules.

Activity A

1 Imagine that you are a builder who has been called in to redesign the kitchen of an Orthodox Jew. Draw a plan of their new kitchen.

2 Add labels and notes to your plan to explain the purpose and design of the kitchen.

Activity B

1 Produce a frequently asked questions (FAQ) page about kosher rules.

2 Think about the things people might want to know, and write them out as questions.

3 Then use the information from this chapter and other sources (for example, the Internet) to answer the questions.

A kosher McDonald's in Tel Aviv, Israel. The fast food firm bowed to pressure from the city's chief rabbi and changed the colour of their trademark signs to assure customers that their burgers and fries are kosher. The McDonald's golden arches have new blue backgrounds, replacing the normal red ones. The signs also display the word 'kosher' in both Hebrew and English.

Many everyday food products carry a label to show that the food is kosher, in the same way that products may also be marked to indicate that they are suitable for vegetarians or Muslims.

- The symbol is usually KLBD which stands for Kosher London Bet Din (Bet Din is a court of Jewish law) or KLBD-D for the kosher dairy products.
- The LBD will have investigated the food products and checked its manufacturing facility, agreeing that it meets the requirements of the kosher rules.
- Another commonly used symbol is a U inside an O and this is from Orthodox Union, based in New York.

A selection of kosher logos that appear on food packaging.

Activity C

1 Investigate how easy it is to buy kosher products in your local stores. You could start by examining the weekly shopping that your family buys.

2 Imagine you are a journalist. Write a review for a Jewish magazine about how easy it is to access kosher food locally.

Activity D

McDonalds in Tel Aviv have made changes to their usual menu to help meet the needs of the Jewish customers is it reasonable then to say:

'Restaurants have a duty to their consumers to develop menus that are accessible to people from different religions and cultural backgrounds'

1 To what extent do you think this is happening in the UK today? Explain reasons for your answer.

2 Do you agree with this statement?

1.6 What happens when Jews are born?

Learning objectives

You will ...
- learn what happens after the birth of a Jewish child
- compare the differences between the birth of a Jewish boy and a Jewish girl
- summarise the reasons why these Jewish ceremonies are important.

A Hebrew name

When a Jewish baby is born he or she is often given a Hebrew name as well as another name. In the Torah, the Hebrew names of many people have a particular meaning or significance. For example, Abraham, who was the founder of Judaism, means 'father of many'. David means 'beloved'; King David led the Israelite people for many years.

The Hebrew names help to link generations together as the tradition is continued. The Hebrew name is also the name that is used in a **Bar** or **Bat Mitzvah** and often on a person's tombstone.

On the Shabbat after the birth of a girl the father is usually asked to read from the Torah in the synagogue, from the bimah. This is a great honour. The name of the baby girl is usually announced and the rabbi will say a blessing for her.

Boys	meaning	Girls	meaning
Aaron	Aaron, the high priest, was Moses' brother	Gila	Joy, happiness
Adin	Gentle, delicate, tender	Idit (Iddit)	Best soil; the best, elite
Haggai	To dance, to celebrate	Levia (Levi'a)	Lioness
Peleg	Brook, creek, stream	Adi	Jewel, ornament
Rahamim (Rachamim)	Compassion, pity, mercy	Doron	Present, gift, offering
Ram	High, tall, lofty; exalted, supreme	Edna	Pleasure, delight

Circumcision

> 'Then God said to Abraham, "As for you, you must keep my covenant … This is my covenant with you and your descendants after you, the covenant you are to keep: Every male among you shall be circumcised … For the generations to come every male among you who is eight days old must be circumcised."'
>
> (Genesis 17:9–12)

In order to fulfil the covenant with God that was first made by Abraham, Jewish boys are circumcised eight days after their birth. This is known as the **Brit Milah**, which means 'the covenant of the cutting'. **Circumcision** is a small operation to remove the flap of skin at the end of the penis. This can be done by a doctor or by a **mohel**. A mohel is a Jew who is specially trained in Jewish circumcision.

Activity A

1 List the people in your class who have names derived from Judaism (e.g. Daniel, Samuel, Jacob, Joshua, Hannah, Sarah, Elizabeth, etc.). Find out more about what each name means.

2 If your class does not have any names derived from Judaism, search the Internet for a Hebrew name that you like. Why did you choose this name?

3 Design a door plaque for a child's room with that name on it. Illustrate the plaque in a way that reflects its meaning.

Activity B

1 In pairs discuss how the celebrations for the birth of a boy compare to the celebrations for the birth of a girl.

2 Consider what makes each type of celebration meaningful and significant.

3 Write a summary of why these celebrations are important. Use your discussion work to help you.

Knowledge check

1 Why are Jewish babies given a Hebrew name as well as another name?

2 What is the name of the ceremony that boys go through at eight days old?

3 Why do boys go through this ceremony?

4 How is the birth of a girl celebrated in a synagogue?

5 What is the difference between a Bar Mitzvah and a Bat Mitzvah?

Activity C

1 Imagine you are the father or mother of a newborn child. Write a diary account about the celebration of your baby's birth. Your account must include a record of the events. Use the information on this page and other sources too, for example the Internet.

2 Your account must also explore the significance and meaning of this event as felt by a Jewish parent.

Activity D

Judaism considers a person Jewish if their mother is Jewish.

Do you agree that a parents culture and religion should have this effect upon the identity of their child?

1.7 How do Jews celebrate Bar or Bat Mitzvah?

Learning objectives

You will …
- learn what happens at Jewish Bar and Bat Mitzvah ceremonies
- understand the meaning of these special ceremonies
- make links between these ceremonies and what you have already learned about Judaism.

In Judaism boys and girls have separate ceremonies to mark the age at which they are considered old enough to take on their religious and moral responsibilities for themselves. Up until this time the parents are expected to make sure that their children perform their religious duties, for example attending the synagogue.

- A boy will go through his ceremony, when he becomes Bar Mitzvah, at the age of thirteen. Bar Mitzvah means 'son of the commandment'.
- Girls are believed to mature earlier than boys and so they take on their religious duties at the age of twelve. The girls' become Bat Mitzvah and this means 'daughter of the commandment'.
- In Progressive synagogues Bar and Bat Mitzvah ceremonies are the same. In an Orthodox synagogue Bar Mitzvah is usually held on the first Shabbat after a boy's thirteenth birthday, and he will read a portion from the Torah. The Bat Mitzvah is usually on a Sunday and, in a Progressive synagogue, the girl will read from the Torah during the service.

Knowledge check

1 What are Bar and Bat Mitzvah ceremonies for?
2 Before these ceremonies take place who is responsible for a child's religious duties?
3 Why do boys and girls have their ceremony at different ages?
4 What is the meaning of the phrases 'Bar Mitzvah' and 'Bat Mitzvah'?
5 How are the ceremonies in Orthodox synagogues different from those in Progressive synagogues?

A girl reads from the Torah at her Bat Mitzvah. Which type of synagogue do you think this is?

I started to prepare for my Bar Mitzvah just after my twelfth birthday. I spent at least two hours a week practising the special prayers that I was going to chant during the service.

The most exciting part of the Bar Mitzvah for me was reading from the Torah. I had to take extra lessons in Hebrew to prepare for my big day. Before the service I was really excited but also quite nervous; I wanted to get everything just right as I celebrated coming of age.

In the Torah God tells us that at the age of thirteen we must take on our own religious responsibility. I want to obey God and follow in the footsteps of many great men of God, like Abraham and Moses.

All my family were at my Bar Mitzvah, of course, as well as lots of my friends, including some who had not been to a synagogue before. After the service we had a party with loads of kosher food and great music.

Ben celebrated becoming Bar Mitzvah last year. He prepares for prayer wearing his prayer shawl which is called a tallit, and his head covering which is called a **kippah**.

Activity A

1 Read what Ben says about his Bar Mitzvah. Make a list of the reasons he gives for why it is important to him.

2 What other examples of keeping mitzvot have you already found out about? In what ways were they similar to this mitzvah?

Activity C

1 Read Ben's account of his Bar Mitzvah.

2 Write an article comparing an Orthodox Jewish girl's Bat Mitzvah to Ben's Bar Mitzvah.

3 Make sure you explain the reasons for the differences as well as describing how an Orthodox Jewish girl might feel during her Bat Mitzvah.

Activity B

1 Make a PowerPoint presentation to explain what happens at a Bar or Bat Mitzvah.

2 You could include the following sections:

   a reasons for having one
   b preparations
   c the actual service
   d the celebrations after the service.

3 Use the information on this page and other sources, for example the Internet, to help you to complete this task.

Activity D

1 In small groups discuss the Jewish belief that girls mature earlier than boys.

2 Make a list of the strengths and weaknesses of having different ages to celebrate their coming of age for religious duties.

3 Hold a class debate and decide whether it is right for Jewish girls to take on their religious responsibilities a year before boys do.

1.8 What festivals do Jews celebrate?

Learning objectives

You will …
- learn about the major festivals in Judaism
- understand why such celebrations are important in Judaism
- predict the effect of these celebrations on family life
- evaluate the importance of remembering significant events in history.

Jewish festivals celebrate many important events from Jewish history. They act as a reminder to the Jews of God's provision for them in the past and his continued involvement in their lives today.

Rosh Hashanah

Rosh Hashanah is the Jewish New Year celebration.

The festival celebrates God's creation of the world and the end of the world when the Day of Judgement will come.

It is a time for fresh starts. Jews will spend ten days reflecting on what they have done wrong and repenting.

It takes place in late September or early October each year.

Jews also accept apologies from each other and end any bad grudges that are being held.

The Jewish calendar starts 3761 years before the Christian calendar. So 2012 is 5773.

Jews hope God will forgive them during this

During Rosh Hashanah the **shofar** is sounded in the synagogue. It has a deep and solemn sound and it reminds Jews that God is almighty and that they must listen to him.

During this festival Jews may send one another cards. On the first evening Jews may dress in new clothes as a sign of the start of a new year and a new beginning. After the service at the festival on the first day Jewish families will usually eat a meal together. They may have apple and honey on the table to wish one another a sweet year ahead. The round apples act as a reminder of the cycle of life. Another traditional food at this time is fish; this symbolises the wish that everyone's goodness will multiply just like the fish in the sea.

The ninth day after Rosh Hashanah is called **Yom Kippur**, which means Day of Atonement. The synagogue service on this evening ends with the reading of the first line of the Shema and the sounding of the shofar.

Pesach

Pesach is a major Jewish festival. It is also known as Passover. Pesach recalls the rescue by God of the Jewish people from slavery in Egypt. This event happened around 1200BCE. During this festival Jews also remember other times when God has saved them from their enemies.

By following God's commands the Jews were set free. Nowadays in the week before Pesach, Jews clean and remove all yeast from their houses, just like the Jews in Egypt. The Jews in Egypt had bread without yeast as there was no time for the bread to rise before they escaped. Families usually play a game and hide ten crumbs containing yeast around the house. The children then have to find the crumbs so that they can be burned. The **Seder** meal on the first night of Pesach is very important. Families try to be together for this.

There is a special order of events for the meal and everyone at the table has a copy of the **Hagadah**. This small booklet helps them to follow the special words for the ceremony. The youngest person at the table asks four questions during the meal and the oldest person answers them. The answers tell the story of the Jews' escape from Egypt. The items on the Sedar plate all have an important significance in this story.

The Jews were slaves in Egypt.

God spoke to Moses through a burning bush and told him he was to lead the Jews to freedom.

Pharaoh refused Moses' request to free the Jews.

God sent nine plagues to Egypt but still the Pharaoh refused.

The night of the tenth plague, the Jews had to take and kill a lamb or goat.

They had to paint lambs' blood on the doorposts.

The Jews had to roast the lamb and eat it with bitter herbs and bread made without yeast.

Any food left was burned and then the Jews had to be dressed ready to travel.

That night the angel of death killed every firstborn child in homes without blood on their doorposts.

That night the Pharaoh's son died and he set the Jews free.

The story of Pesach.

The table is laid with a white tablecloth and two candles. Cushions are put on chairs to give people comfort, a reminder of the freedom they have, unlike the slaves.

Everyone has a wine glass and an extra one is put on the table for the **Prophet** Elijah. Jews believe that Elijah will one day return from Heaven to announce the coming of the Jewish saviour. Wine is used to remember God's promises to rescue his people and ten drips of wine are made on a napkin to recall the ten plagues. Matzah, which is bread without yeast, is placed on the table. Also on the table is a small bowl of salt water, which is a reminder of the tears of the slaves. Parsley is dipped in this. In the centre of the table is the Sedar plate.

The final words said at the end of the Sedar meal are, 'Next year in Jerusalem.'

Roasted egg: a reminder of new life and sacrifices made in the past at the temple.

Shankbone: a reminder of the lamb.

Parsley: a reminder that God cared for the Jews when they left Egypt.

Charoset: a paste made of fruits and nuts. It is symbolic of cement used by the slaves when building the pyramids. It also represents the sweetness of the Jews' freedom.

The Sedar meal.

Knowledge check

Read pages 24–27.

1 During which festival do Jews celebrate New Year?

2 In what way is this festival a time for looking backwards?

3 At the New Year celebration what are Jews remembering?

4 What does the sounding of the shofar remind Jews of?

5 What might be eaten during the final meal of this celebration?

6 What does Pesach help the Jews to remember?

7 What causes the Pharaoh to finally release the Jews?

8 What is the name of the most important meal in this celebration?

9 List the symbolic foods in this meal and say what each represents.

10 How is the story of the Jews' escape from Egypt retold during this meal?

Activity A

1 Create a summary information page to tell your peers about how either Rosh Hashanah or Pesach are celebrated.

2 You should use both text and images to communicate the information.

Activity B

1 List ways in which thinking about mistakes made in the past year may help a person in their next year.

2 Create a card that a Jew could send at Rosh Hashanah that focuses on forgiveness and the hope for a new year.

Activity C

All Jewish festivals involve the whole family. Often this may include a meal that contains symbolic items, readings or actions.

1 In small groups, discuss the effect that religious celebrations may have on a Jewish family.

2 List the positive outcomes that you think all families could benefit from.

3 Create a poster that promotes some of these positive outcomes of spending times of celebration together.

Activity D

Rosh Hashanah and Pesach demonstrate that Jewish festivals recall important events from Jewish history. There are other major celebrations in Judaism too; these include **Shavuot**, **Sukkot**, **Hanukkah** and **Purim**.

1 In small groups, each choose one of the festivals listed above.

2 Each person in the group should research what that festival is celebrating and how Jews celebrate it.

3 Each person should present their research using PowerPoint.

4 In your groups, create a list of reasons why remembering events from the past is a helpful thing and why it may be an unhelpful thing.

5 Hold a class debate and decide whether celebrating the past is helpful to living in the present.

The big assignment

Task

To produce a multimedia publicity campaign aimed at encouraging young Jews to remain committed to their beliefs.

Objectives

- To research what it means to be Jewish.
- To consider the challenges Judaism faces in the UK.
- To suggest reasons why keeping mitzvot in a non-Jewish culture is important.

Outcome

To produce a multimedia publicity campaign that could be used in the UK to help encourage and support young Jews to remain committed to their faith.

You should include information about:

- kosher eating
- celebrating Shabbat
- Bar and Bat Mitzvah
- learning Hebrew
- attending the synagogue.

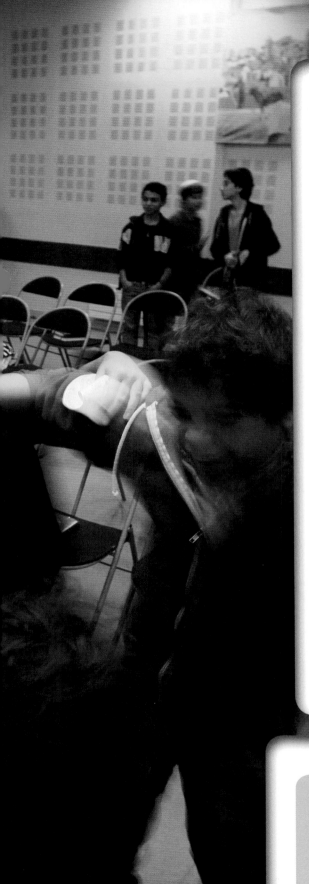

Guidance

1. Work in groups of six people. Each person should be given a specific job to do, and the rest of the group should support them in doing it.

2. Pupils who are Jewish could act as advisors to the groups.

3. Take one topic each and conduct some thorough factual research.

4. Think about possible problems a Jew may face following this aspect of their religion in the UK today.

5. Think of ways that positive elements of this aspect of their faith could be highlighted and promoted.

6. Each member of the group should produce a summary of their work to share with the group.

7. As a group decide on the form of publicity that will be produced for each section of the project. For example, you may choose to create flyers on kosher food, including great places to eat, a TV advert about Shabbat and the importance of family time, and a radio advert about attending a synagogue. Each person should then complete their piece of publicity based upon their summary sheet of information and ideas.

8. Include persuasive language and engaging visual images and presentations. Have a look at advertising that you like and see if you can apply some of the same ideas to your own work.

9. Your completed publicity pack should contain a range of media: film, radio, newspaper articles, posters and flyers.

10. Present your final pack either to the local rabbi or to your RE teacher and ask for their feedback. You could also ask the head of business studies to feedback to you on the quality of your publicity/advertising.

11. As a group, evaluate your pack. Decide what you did well and how you could have improved it.

Assessment

You will be assessed on:

✓ how well you use specialist vocabulary

✓ your ability to explain the importance of young Jews remaining faithful

✓ your ability to show empathy with young Jews in Britain.

✓ the accuracy of your accounts of Jewish practices.

2.1 What do Jews believe about God?

Learning objectives

You will … • learn what Jews believe about God because of his titles
• understand what the Torah reveals about God
• interpret the significance of God's holiness for the Jewish people.

God's name is considered absolutely holy by the Jews.

- Jews say God (it is not a name) but write G_d.
- YHWH is the name of God used in the Tenakh. It is usually pronounced Yahweh. This name means 'I am'. This is a reminder to the Jews that God is **eternal**, and it is he who creates all living things. Jews do not say the name Yahweh, but replace it with **adonai** (Lord) in speech and LORD (upper case letters) when written.
- Much of God's character is also revealed by the titles that he is given throughout the books of the Tenakh (on the right).

The most important statement of belief in Judaism is the Shema (see page 6).

- Shema means 'hear' and it is taken from the first word in the statement, which is 'Hear O Israel, the Lord our God is one God' (Deuteronomy 6:4).
- This belief is central to Judaism. Judaism is a monotheistic religion, meaning that Jews believe in and worship only one God.
- They are reminded of the oneness of their God throughout the day in their prayers and through their daily commitment to mitzvah.

Elohim (authority)
אלהים

El (mighty one)
אל

Shaddai (almighty)
אלשדי

Adonai (master)
ארבי

Elyon (most high)
עליון

Avinu (our father)
מַלְכֵּנוּ

Hebrew titles given to God.

Knowledge check

1. In the Tenakh what name is God known by?
2. Why is his name sometimes written as 'G_d' in English?
3. What does God's name remind Jews about his character?
4. Why can Judaism be described as a monotheistic religion?
5. How does the way Jews keep mitzvot remind them of the oneness of God? You may need to look back at your previous work on Judaism to answer this question.

> 'In the beginning God created the heavens and the earth.'
> (Genesis 1:1)

> ‘"Who can hide in secret places so that I cannot see them?" declares the LORD. "Do not I fill heaven and earth?" declares the LORD.'
> (Jeremiah 23:24)

> ‘"Now if you obey me fully and keep my covenant, then out of all nations you will be my treasured possession. Although the whole earth is mine, you will be a holy nation."'
> (Exodus 19:5–6)

> ‘"I am the LORD, who brought you up out of Egypt to be your God; therefore be holy, because I am holy."'
> (Leviticus 11:45)

Activity A

Look at the various titles God is given in Hebrew on page 30.

1 In pairs discuss what the titles tell you about the God of the Jews.

2 Summarise what you can say about the nature of God based upon the titles that he is given in Hebrew.

3 Create a poster to illustrate three of the Hebrew titles for God. Include the Hebrew names on your poster too. You could try to write them in Hebrew script.

Activity B

1 In pairs discuss what the above quotations from the Torah reveal about Jewish beliefs about God.

2 Create an advert revealing these Jewish beliefs about God.

3 You need to decide what form your advert will take. For example, you could do a billboard poster, a TV or radio advert or a flyer.

Activity C

1 In pairs discuss how the belief about God as creator, in Genesis 1:1, may affect Jewish behaviour and lifestyles.

2 What causes you to come up with these suggestions?

3 Carry out further research to confirm whether your initial suggestions were correct. You may find the Internet a useful resource.

4 Present your findings in the form of a brief guide for Jews on how to behave because of the belief that God is the creator of all things.

Activity D

In the Talmud it asks the question, 'What does it mean "You shall walk after the Lord your God"?' (Deuteronomy 13:4).

1 In pairs discuss reasons why this question may have been asked. Record your answers on a spidergram.

2 What answers can you and your classmate come up with for the question asked in the Talmud?

3 Rank your answers by placing a number 1 next to the one you believe to be the strongest reason, and so on.

4 Explain why you have ranked your answers in this order.

2.2 Who was Abraham?

Learning objectives

You will …
- learn about the life of Abraham
- understand why Abraham is important to Jews
- deduce what kind of relationship Abraham's life causes there to be between Jews and Muslims today.

This is the story of **Abraham** as told in the Torah. Abraham was originally called Abram. He lived in Ur, which is now part of Iraq, before travelling to Haran with his family. His father was called Terah.

At this time people believed in many gods. This is known as **polytheism**. Abram's father sold **idols** too (sculptures of gods). In the **Midrash** there are stories about Abraham smashing his father's idols when he realises that there can be only one God of heaven and earth. It is this one God whom Abram begins to worship. This is the start of Judaism as a monotheistic religion.

God calls Abram to leave his home to follow him. In Genesis 12, God promises Abram that he will be his God, that Abram will have many descendants and that he will deliver God and his people into a promised land. God promised to set apart the Hebrews as his chosen people. This is the start of the **covenant** between God and the Jewish people.

Abram was married to Sarai but they had no children. As they were growing old Abram was worried that he had no one to follow on after him, despite God's promise. Sarai gave her maid servant, Hagar, as a wife to Abram. She became pregnant and Abram had a son called Ishmael, who, according to both Muslim and Jewish tradition, is the ancestor of the Arabs.

God then promised Abram and Sarai a son. He also changed their names: Abram became Abraham, meaning 'father of many' and Sarai became Sarah, which means 'princess'. Despite Abraham being 100 years old and Sarah being 90 they did have a son. Their son was named Isaac and he is the ancestor of the Jewish people. By giving him his son Isaac, God begins to fulfil his promise to Abraham that he will have many descendants.

'Sarah and the angels' by contemporary
Jewish artist Richard McBee.

Abraham leaves his home when God tells him to, without knowing where he is going. Abraham obeys God in all that he is told to do.

For example, in Genesis 22, God tells Abraham to kill his own son, Isaac, on a sacrificial altar. Abraham obeys God and prepares to sacrifice his son. However, when he raises his knife God tells him to stop. God tests Abraham's faithfulness and obedience and Abraham passes these tests.

The blessings of God to the Jewish people are passed on from Abraham, through his descendants, right up to the present-day Jews. Jews today believe that God still cares for them and that they remain his special people.

A 13th-century illustration of Abraham preparing to sacrifice Isaac. An angel of God is stopping him.

Knowledge check

1 How was Abram's monotheistic faith different from other religious beliefs at that time?

2 What did Abram's father do?

3 What covenant did God make with Abram?

4 When did God change Abram's name to Abraham?

5 Describe one way in which God tested Abraham's faith.

6 How is God's blessing to Abraham passed on to Jews today?

Activity A

1 Summarise the life story of Abraham using five pictures and write a caption to go with each one.

2 Find another example of how God tested Abraham's faith. You will need to do some research to complete this task.

3 Explain this example in your own words.

Activity B

1 Design a questionnaire to find out why Abraham is such an important person in Judaism.

2 You will need to think of questions you could ask based on the information on pages 32–34.

3 Once your questionnaire is designed you should then complete it with answers to the questions that you think a Jew would give.

Muslims and Jews in the Middle East. What links these two religions together?

Activity C

1 In small groups discuss what lessons can be learned from the life of Abraham.

2 Is there anything that could be useful to all people?

3 Write a guide called 'Lessons from Abraham'. Include handy tips for living that could help all people. Use your discussion work to help you to complete this task.

Activity D

Islam and Judaism both believe in Abraham. Through Abraham, Jews believe God has blessed them. Muslims believe God gave them their most important messenger, the Prophet Muhammad, through Abraham.

1 In small groups discuss what effect you would expect this shared religious background to have on relationships between Muslims and Jews.

2 Write a list summarising your discussion. Make sure you give reasons for each idea that you have come up with.

3 Research the relationships between Jews and Muslims in the Middle East at this current time. How does it compare to your expectations?

4 Produce a short film that brings together your research.

Learning objectives

You will ...
- learn how Judaism developed, beginning with Abraham
- understand why Jerusalem is important to the Jews
- understand how the State of Israel was established.

Judaism came from God's promise to Abraham that his descendants would become the holy nation of Israel.

Through Abraham's son Isaac, the prophet and leader of the Jewish people, Moses, was born.

The Jews were to be holy, to serve God and follow his commands. Jews believe that God brought them through many troubled times, including freeing them from slavery in Egypt. God promised the Jews a land of their own; this land was to be Israel, and at its centre was the holy city of **Jerusalem**.

The Wailing Wall (also called the Western Wall) in Jerusalem. Why do you think this wall was given this name? Can you find out more about the Wailing Wall and its significance to Jews today?

Jerusalem

The Jewish nation became strong and was led by many kings, including Solomon who was the first to build the Temple in Jerusalem for God. The Temple was the focus for all Jewish worship and it was a reminder of God's presence among them. However, in 586BCE the Temple was destroyed by the Babylonians and many Jews were taken into exile in Babylon (present-day Iraq). In 538BCE work on rebuilding the Temple began and many Jews returned from exile. The Jews who chose not to return were the start of the **Diaspora**.

Eventually in 63BCE the Romans took over Jerusalem and the influence of the Jews was weakened. Over time the Jews became more spread out and the Temple became less of a focus for worship; many synagogues had been set up. After Jesus' birth, life and death some Jews believed he rose from the dead and he was the **Messiah**. Those who followed Jesus as the Messiah later became known as Christians.

In 70CE and again in 132CE the Jews revolted against the Romans. Both times the Temple was destroyed. The Temple has never been rebuilt; all that remains is the Wailing Wall.

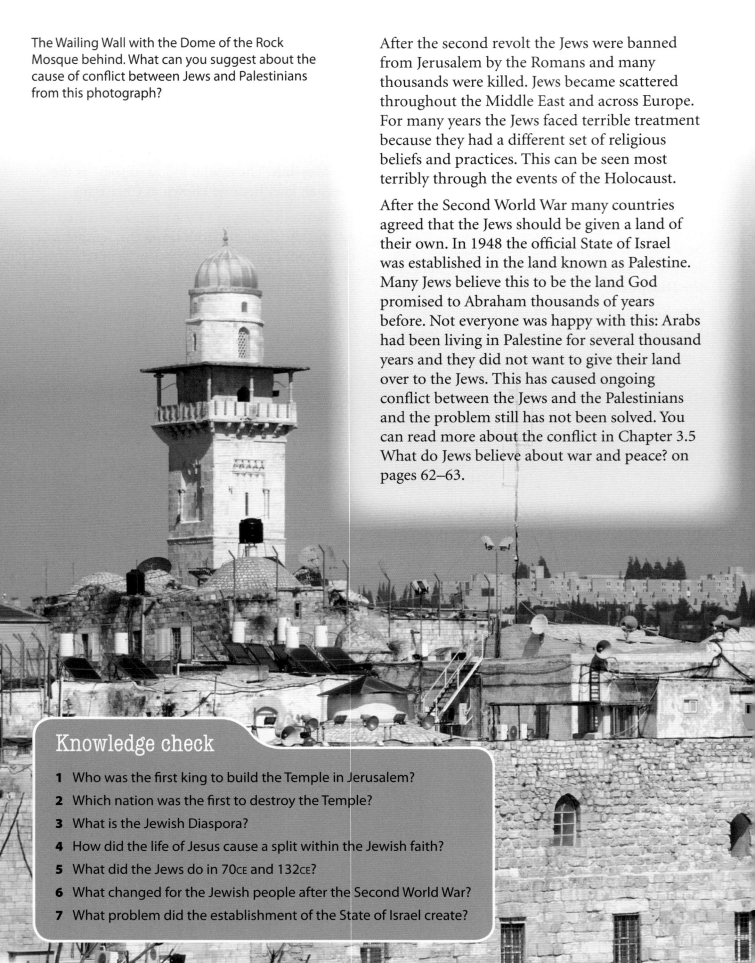

The Wailing Wall with the Dome of the Rock Mosque behind. What can you suggest about the cause of conflict between Jews and Palestinians from this photograph?

After the second revolt the Jews were banned from Jerusalem by the Romans and many thousands were killed. Jews became scattered throughout the Middle East and across Europe. For many years the Jews faced terrible treatment because they had a different set of religious beliefs and practices. This can be seen most terribly through the events of the Holocaust.

After the Second World War many countries agreed that the Jews should be given a land of their own. In 1948 the official State of Israel was established in the land known as Palestine. Many Jews believe this to be the land God promised to Abraham thousands of years before. Not everyone was happy with this: Arabs had been living in Palestine for several thousand years and they did not want to give their land over to the Jews. This has caused ongoing conflict between the Jews and the Palestinians and the problem still has not been solved. You can read more about the conflict in Chapter 3.5 What do Jews believe about war and peace? on pages 62–63.

Knowledge check

1 Who was the first king to build the Temple in Jerusalem?
2 Which nation was the first to destroy the Temple?
3 What is the Jewish Diaspora?
4 How did the life of Jesus cause a split within the Jewish faith?
5 What did the Jews do in 70CE and 132CE?
6 What changed for the Jewish people after the Second World War?
7 What problem did the establishment of the State of Israel create?

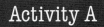

Activity A

1. Create a timeline that marks the main events in Jewish history.
2. For each event add a fact box and an illustration.
3. You can use the information in this chapter as well as carrying out additional research using the Internet.

Activity B

1. Create a booklet that explains the importance of Jerusalem to the Jews.
2. In your booklet include:
   - a labelled plan of the Temple before its destruction – to do this you will need to find out more about the Temple
   - an explanation of the significance of the Wailing Wall
   - an account of the establishment of the State of Israel in 1948.

Activity C

1. In small groups discuss why you think it is not easy for Jews and Arabs to live peacefully in Israel today.
2. Discuss and then list ways that the two groups might resolve the problems that they face. Share your conclusions with the whole class.

Activity D

The Jews have faced many hard times in their history. Find out more about the Crusades and how they contributed to **anti-Semitism**. Put together a PowerPoint presentation of your findings.

2.4 Are all Jews the same?

Learning objectives

You will ...
- learn about the differences between Orthodox and Progressive Jews
- understand the reasons for the differences within Judaism
- evaluate the effects of the differences within Judaism.

There are many branches of Judaism and each branch follows their beliefs in a slightly different way. These differences happen because of the way each group interprets the Torah. Two main branches of Judaism are the Progressive Jews and Orthodox Jews.

Progressive Jews

Progressive Jews seek to modernise their faith, making it move with the times. Outwardly, Progressive Jews look no different from anybody else. They do not follow religious rules that affect their outward appearance.

In the synagogue men and women have an equal role in worship. Men and women may sit together during worship. Both men and women can be **rabbis**. Rabbi means 'my teacher'. Rabbis lead worship in the synagogue.

Orthodox Jews

Orthodox Jews are far more traditional in the way that they follow their religion. These Jews follow their religion as strictly as possible. For some Orthodox Jews this includes wearing a style of clothing that has remained unchanged since the nineteenth century.

In the Torah men lead worship and so in the synagogue only men can be rabbis or read from the Torah. Men and women will also sit separately during worship so that they can remain focused upon worshipping God. Orthodox Jews believe it would be wrong to change the way they follow the rules of God. Such disobedience is unacceptable to them.

Knowledge check

1. Why are there different branches within Judaism?

2. What are two examples of different types of Judaism?

3. What do Progressive Jews try to do to their religion?

4. Give one example of the way Progressive Jews demonstrate this in the synagogue.

5. In what way do Orthodox Jews try to follow their religion?

6. Give one example of how Orthodox Jews demonstrate this in the synagogue.

7. Why do Orthodox Jews believe it is wrong to try to modernise their faith?

Are all Jews the same?

Activity A

1 From the photographs on this page, who can you identify as Jewish? What clues in the pictures enabled you to identify the faith of these people?

2 Are there any people whose religion you cannot identify? Why is this?

3 What reasons can you give for why some Jews demonstrate their faith through their appearance while others do not?

Jewish beliefs

Activity B

1 In pairs discuss how you could divide up the Jewish beliefs shown on the spidergram on the right.

2 Draw a Venn diagram to show the Progressive and Orthodox beliefs. Where do they overlap?

3 Add to your diagram other similarities or differences you are aware of through your previous work on Judaism.

Activity C

1 In small groups discuss the reason for the differences between Progressive and Orthodox Jews.

2 Create a see-saw diagram (like the one below) to help you evaluate the views of both Orthodox Jews and Progressive Jews.

3 Which approach to the Jewish faith do you most agree with? Give reasons for your answer.

4 Explain why you think the opposing approach is weaker.

There is only one God and he alone should be worshipped.

Men and women have equal roles within religion.

Worship must follow exactly the rules given in the Torah.

Jewish Beliefs

Judaism must change to fit in with society.

It is unrealistic to follow every rule in the Torah in the modern world.

God is the creator of all things.

To obey God you should follow Orthodox Judaism

Agree   **Disagree**

Activity D

The quotation, 'United we stand, divided we fall' comes from a traditional fable.

1 In small groups discuss what you think this quotation means.

2 Can you think of examples that would demonstrate that this idea has some truth in it?

3 Discuss whether you think the divisions within Judaism are a good thing or whether such divisions may weaken their religion.

4 Imagine the local rabbi has asked you to report your findings back to him or her. Write a letter that summarises the contents of your discussion and the conclusion that you have reached.

2.5 What do Jews believe about life after death?

Learning objectives

You will ...
- learn about what happens at Jewish funerals
- make links between Jewish mourning and Jewish beliefs about life after death
- assess the importance for religions of having clear teachings about the afterlife.

Jews believe that our time on Earth is just one phase in our soul's existence. For Jews their true spiritual home is not on Earth.

However, during their time on Earth Jews believe they are taking part in God's plan, as many generations before them have done. Death moves a person's soul onto the next phase in life. In some ways Jews believe everything is known and planned by God: death when it comes is part of this plan.

Funerals

- *'For dust you are, and to dust you will return.'* (Genesis 3:19). Orthodox Jews take this quotation to mean that a body should be buried and not cremated.
- A funeral is arranged as soon as possible after death, ideally within 24 hours.
- The funeral service is led by the rabbi. During the funeral, prayers are said. Close relatives will rip the lapels of their clothes to show symbolically how their lives have been torn by grief.
- As the coffin is lowered into the ground Psalm 91 is said. This Psalm focuses on God as the protector: *'I will say of the LORD, "He is my refuge and my fortress, my God, in whom I trust."'* (Psalm 91:2).
- In Israel the body is simply wrapped in a **shroud** before being laid into the ground. This is so the body touches the ground as the Torah says it should.
- A special prayer is said called the **Kaddish**. The Kaddish praises God as the Creator. Everyone then throws a spade of dirt into the grave. This action demonstrates that they have accepted the death. Afterwards the mourners wash their hands to symbolise the separation between life and death.

- On the day of the funeral seven days of mourning begin. This is called **shiva**. The mourners will do nothing in this time that involves comfort or pleasure; their time is spent grieving for their loved one. A special candle, called a **Yahrzeit** candle, burns throughout these seven days.
- For 30 days after this the mourners will continue to avoid all entertainment.
- Close relatives may mourn for a further eleven months until the first anniversary of the death.
- On the anniversary of the death a Yahrzeit candle is lit and the Kaddish is recited again. This is to celebrate the deceased person's ongoing existence outside this world.

The Yahrzeit candle is a reminder of the Jewish proverb that says, 'A person's soul is the candle of the Lord.' This is a modern electric one.

Knowledge check

1 According to Judaism who plans everything that happens in life, including death?

2 What do Orthodox Jews understand from the quotation in Genesis 3:19?

3 How many hours after death does a Jewish funeral take place?

4 What do the words in Psalm 91 focus the mourners' thoughts on as the coffin is lowered into the ground?

5 What is the name of the prayer said at the graveside?

6 What are the seven days of mourning called?

7 What does the Yahrzeit candle remind the mourners of?

8 What is celebrated a year after the person's death?

Activity A

1 In pairs discuss and then list all the things that happen at a Jewish funeral and during mourning.

2 In a parallel column identify beliefs about death and the afterlife that are associated with each of these events.

3 Discuss how you think this process helps the mourners. Record your ideas on a spidergram and then share them with the rest of the class.

Activity B

During shiva Jews avoid all pleasure and comfort.

1 In pairs discuss what effect this would actually have on a person's life.

2 Imagine you are going through a time of shiva. Write a diary account of one day during this period.

3 To develop your answer use the information provided on this page and carry out additional research (for example, using the Internet) about shiva.

Life after death

Judaism focuses mainly on living correctly for God in this life. Judaism doesn't have many specific teachings on what will happen after death. It is however clear in the Tenakh that life does continue after death in some form.

The life to come is called **Olam Ha-Ba** in Hebrew. Life after death for the righteous followers of Judaism is often called Gan Eden, meaning the Garden of Eden. The Talmud uses images of golden furniture, including stools and great banquet tables, to show the righteous celebrating Shabbat and enjoying sunshine.

There is also an idea of some kind of punishment which includes a person being cut off from his own people. This is shown in Daniel 12:2 which says:

'Multitudes who sleep [this means those who are dead] *in the dust of the earth will awake: some to everlasting life, others to shame and everlasting contempt* [disrespect].'

When Jews visit a grave, they leave a stone on it to show that the person has not been forgotten.

Activity C

A **Mishnah** passage says, 'This world is like a lobby before the Olam Ha-Ba. Prepare yourself in the lobby so that you may enter the banquet hall.'

1 Discuss in pairs what you think this quotation means.

2 Create a spidergram to record how you think a Jew prepares in this life to enter the afterlife as a righteous person. Think back over the work you have already done to help you complete this task.

3 Create a collage or a mural that illustrates the way Jews live now in preparation for the afterlife.

Activity D

1 In small groups discuss whether you think it is important for a religion to have clear teachings on the afterlife.

2 What are the possible effects on believers of not having clear teachings about the afterlife within their religion? Remember to use your knowledge of Judaism to help inform your thinking.

3 Hold a class debate on the importance of a religion having clear teachings about the afterlife.

2.6 What do Jews believe about creation and science?

Learning objectives

You will ...
- learn about Jewish beliefs about creation
- find out why there are differences within Jewish beliefs
- evaluate the account of creation that is in the Torah.

The first book in the Torah is Genesis. In Genesis it describes how God created the earth and everything on it in six days. On the seventh day the account says that God rested.

On the Jewish calendar the year represents the number of years since creation. This has been done by adding up the ages of people in the Torah, right back to the time of creation. In 2012 the Jewish year was 5773.

> 'And God said, "Let there be light," and there was light.'
>
> (Genesis 1:3)

This quotation from Genesis 1 explains that God created things by speaking; by calling them into existence. Everything God created over the six days was declared as being 'very good'.

Jews read in the Torah that the first man God created was Adam. God gives Adam the job of naming all the animals. Later in Genesis humans are given the responsibility of ruling over the animals and caring for the earth. Jews believe that this remains the responsibility of humans today.

Day 1   Day 4
Day 2   Day 5
Day 3   Day 6

The story of creation.

Knowledge check

1. How many days did God take to create the world?
2. After creating the world what does Genesis say that God did?
3. How does this account say that God created the world?
4. Who was the first human to be created in the Genesis account?
5. What responsibilities do Jews believe that God gave humans once he had finished creating the world?

Some Jews, for example Orthodox Jews, accept the Torah as being God's words. For Orthodox Jews the Torah is absolutely true and correct, there are no mistakes in it. For these Jews the Genesis account of creation is accurate and they hold the belief that God did indeed create the earth in six days. Many Orthodox Jews acknowledge that the six 'days' are not 24-hour days, but time periods.

For other Jews, for example Progressive Jews, the Genesis account is not meant to be taken as an actual story of what happened during creation. The story is understood in a more symbolic way. This means that some Jews believe the story was written to help them to understand that God was the creator. However, the way in which he created the world in the story is simply symbolic. Progressive Jews may choose to believe other ideas about how the world began. For example, they may agree with scientific ideas that suggest a big explosion at the start of time led to the development of the world. They may choose to believe this because of the scientific evidence that is used to support this idea.

Activity A

1 Create a diagram to explain what happened on the six days of creation.

2 Interpret the images depicting each of the days to help you. You may also find it useful to look up the account in Genesis.

Activity B

1 In small groups discuss the Genesis account of creation. What questions could you ask about this account? As a group record your questions on a large spidergram.

2 Using your questions to guide you, discuss of any parts of the account that you find hard to accept.

3 Share your ideas with the rest of the class.

Activity C

1 What three arguments could you give to support the Orthodox belief that God really did create the world in six days? It may be helpful to consider what you know about Jewish beliefs about God to help you.

2 What three arguments could you give to support the view that the creation story is symbolic and that science tells us how the world came to exist? It may be helpful to carry out more research into scientific ideas about how the world began.

Activity D

1 Create a newspaper article to discuss whether the account in Genesis should be accepted as factual.

2 In your article you first need to present the account given in Genesis chapter 1 in your own words.

3 Next you must explain why some people, including some Jews, may find this difficult to accept as a factual account.

4 Finally, present your view on whether the Genesis account should be taken as fact or whether you think there is a stronger argument for how the world began.

5 Make sure you give reasons for the opinions that you include in your newspaper article.

The big assignment

Task

To produce an information pack to provide people with an overview of Jewish beliefs.

Objectives

- To identify the level of knowledge about Judaism in your local community in order to inform the content of your information pack.

- To research a number of topics to give an overview of the main Jewish beliefs.

- To effectively present your findings for your local community.

Outcome

To produce an information pack that provides non-Jewish people in your local community with greater information about Jewish beliefs.

You should include information about:

- life after death

- creation

- God

- Abraham

- differences within Judaism.

Guidance

1   Work in groups of six people. Each person should be given a specific job to do, and the rest of the group should support them in carrying it out.

2   Suggested jobs:

   a   Create a questionnaire to find out what non-Jewish people in your local community already know about Jewish beliefs. Get a range of people in the local community to complete the questionnaire.

   b   Write down some questions that you could ask local Jews in order to find out about their beliefs.

   c   Interview some Jews and write up their answers.

   d   Find out evidence for Jewish teachings on the topics through research on the Internet and at the library.

   e   Take photographs or find relevant illustrations to go with the information.

   f   Plan what your information pack is going to include. You may consider having a series of leaflets, one for each topic, as well as an information poster.

3   As a group go through the material gathered – i.e. the outcomes of each job – and for each one decide what needs to be done to make use of it in the pack.

4   Your completed information pack should contain a series of leaflets that include written information, images and possibly quotations from Jewish people who you have interviewed.

5   Present your information pack to the leader of the local council, the manager of the local community centre or another community leader and ask for their feedback.

6   As a group, evaluate your information pack. Decide what you did well and what you could have done to improve it.

Assessment

You will be assessed on:

✓ how well you use specialist vocabulary

✓ your ability to explain the religious beliefs

✓ your ability to create a pack that meets the needs of your local community.

3.1 What guides Jewish morality?

Learning objectives

You will ...
- find out about the Aseret ha-D'varimthe and how it guides Jews in their moral decisions
- decide how a Jew would answer particular moral questions
- evaluate the content of the Aseret ha-D'varimthe.

A **halakhic** life means a life of walking with God. This is the kind of life Jews seek to live. Walking with God means following his ways and obeying his commands so that in all they do Jews are aiming to behave as God wants them to.

The main guidance for living is found in the ten statements, given by God to Moses and in the 613 mitzvot. These commands are there to guide Jews in their journey through life and to help them walk with God.

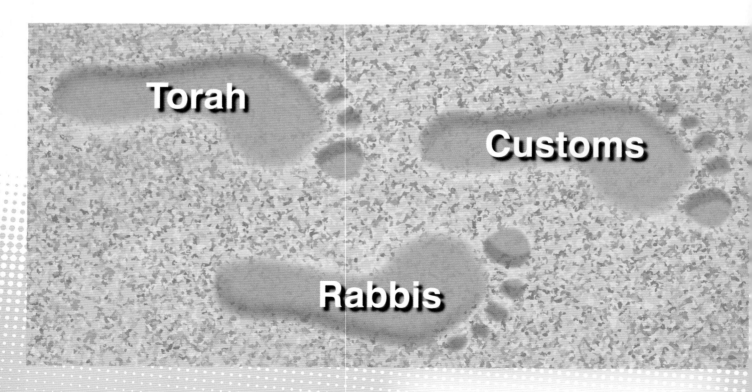

The Halakhah is made up of three sources, and laws from any of these sources are equally important and to be observed.

Generally, Jews follow the law of the country that they are living in. If they have concerns about a matter, for example Jewish divorce or food rules, they can go to the Bet Din. The Bet Din is a special Jewish court made up of three rabbis. The only country in the world that is governed by the Jewish law code, the Halakhah, is Israel.

The Bet Din is a special Jewish court made up of three rabbis. This one is in Israel.

The Ten Aseret ha-D'varimthe

The account in Exodus 20 tells how Moses brought down from Mount Sinai two stone tablets. The Torah says that on them was recorded the ten Aseret ha-D'varimthe. When translated Aseret ha-D'varimthe means the Ten Sayings or the Ten Declarations. Christians call them the Ten Commandments. These ten declarations are not seen as individual commandments in Judaism; rather they are categories of mitzvot. Each of the 613 mitzvot can be placed under one of these ten categories. For example, one Jewish mitzvah says that a person should not to stand aside while a person's life is in danger. It fits somewhat obviously into the category against murder.

1 Belief in God
'I am the Lord, your God ...'

2 Forbidding improper worship
'You shall not have other gods ...'

3 Forbidding promises
'You shall not take the name of the Lord your God in vain ...'

4 Observing holy times
'Remember the Sabbath day ...'

5 Respect for parents and teachers
'Honour your father and mother ...'

The ten categories are based on the account of the stone tablets given in Exodus 20:2–14.

Activity A

1 Create a poster with ten pairs of footprints on it.

2 In one footprint write a category from the Aseret ha-D'varimthe.

3 In the footprint next to it write an example of a behaviour or act that would reflect that Aseret ha-D'varimthe. For example, next to the Aseret ha-D'varimthe that says 'Forbidding harming a person through speech', you may write 'Do not lie'.

Activity B

1 In small groups discuss one of the following issues:

   a   divorce
   b   stealing
   c   lying.

2 Based on the Aseret ha-D'varimthe what do you think a Jew would believe about that issue? Why?

3 Create a role play to demonstrate how a Jew would react to the issue that you have been dealing with.

4 Perhaps try to find out more about the Jewish law on the issue that your group has chosen to help you develop your role play. Use other sources such as the Internet to inform your research.

6   Forbidding physically harming a person
'You shall not murder.'

7   Forbidding sexual immorality
'You shall not commit adultery.'

8   Forbidding theft
'You shall not steal.'

9   Forbidding harming a person through speech
'You shall not bear false witness against your neighbour.'

10   Forbidding coveting
'You shall not covet your neighbour's house ...'

Activity C

In small groups create a 'problem page' for young Jews. You should try to include:

1 Letters to the problem page that present at least three different moral dilemmas

2 Include answers to the letters that offer advice based on the Aseret ha D'Varimthe and any other relevant mitzvot that you wish to include.

Activity D

- In pairs discuss the ten categories in the Aseret ha D'Varimthe and rank them in the order you think they should be in. Place the most important one at the top of the list.
- Make sure that you have reasons for the order that you have put them in.
- Discuss whether you would add any extra categories to the list.
- Hold a class discussion to find out what changes your class would make to the order and content of the Aseret ha-D'varimthe.

3.2 How do Jews treat the world around them?

Learning objectives

You will ...
- understand Jewish teachings about stewardship
- learn how Jews put their beliefs about the environment into practice.

In the book of Genesis it says that God created the world and all the creatures on earth. In Genesis God declares his creation good. God gives humans the responsibility of caring for his creation, both the planet and the animals on it. This responsibility given to humans by God is called **stewardship**.

As stewards, Jews believe that they must:

- **Protect and conserve the natural world**
  An example of this is the Noah Project. This group was formed by British Jews in 1997. They work on practical projects and give 10 per cent of their profits to environmental work.
- **Reduce their carbon footprint**
  An example of this is the Big Green Jewish Campaign: Year of the Bagel, a whole year of campaigns, action and education focusing on the way Jews understand the world and impact on the environment. In 2011 the campaign focused on food and encouraging Jews to eat locally sourced kosher produce.
- **Increase sustainability**
  An example of this can be seen through the work of COEJL (Coalition on the Environment and Jewish Life) which has worked with the No Impact Project in the USA to change people's lifestyles and to make greater use of green energy.

Activity A

1 Choose one area of environmental concern listed on the left.

2 Create a leaflet that explains this environmental concern and provides examples of how Jewish people are working responsibly for the environment in this area.

3 Complete this task using the information in this chapter and through additional research, for example the Internet.

Activity B

1 Create a poster that promotes the Jewish teachings about caring for the environment.

2 Include some Jewish quotations on your poster.

3 Suggest some things people could do to support the Jewish belief that we should all care for our world.

Knowledge check

1 Why do Jews believe that they have a responsibility to care for the earth?

2 What word is used to describe this responsibility?

3 Give an example of one thing a Jew may try to do in order to care for the environment.

'The world and all that is in it belong to the Lord; the earth and all who live on it are his.'

(Psalm 24)

'God said: "Look at my creations! See how beautiful and perfect they are! … Make sure you don't ruin or destroy My world."'

(**Midrash** Kohelet (Ecclesiastes) Rabbah 7:20)

'God blessed them and God said to them, "… fill the earth and subdue it; and rule over the fish of the sea, the bird in the sky, and every living thing that moves on earth."'

(Genesis 1:28)

Tu B'Shevat is the Jewish 'New Year for Trees'. It takes place on the fifteenth day of the Jewish month of Shevat. On Tu B'Shevat Jews celebrate the gifts of the natural world.

Tu B'Shevat marks the beginning of spring in Israel. At this time there is usually plenty of rain and the earth responds with new life springing up all around.

To mark Tu B'Shevat, schoolchildren in Israel plant trees. Often these trees have been provided by the contributions of Jews from around the world who collect money to send to Israel for this festival.

Activity C

1 In pairs read each of the quotations on the right. Discuss what you think each one means.

2 Write a parable to help to teach younger children the Jewish belief that the world belongs to God and that humans are only stewards and not owners of it.

Activity D

1 Work in pairs to produce a PowerPoint presentation about the Jewish festival of Tu B'Shevat.

2 You will need to find out more about the origins and celebrations of this festival.

3 In your presentation explain how this festival demonstrates a recognition of God as creator and owner of the world the Jewish understanding of stewardship.

4 Do you think such festivals have a lasting impact upon how people treat the environment on a day to day basis? Write a paragraph explaining what you think.

Planting trees for Tu B'Shevat.

3.3 What do Jews believe about family life?

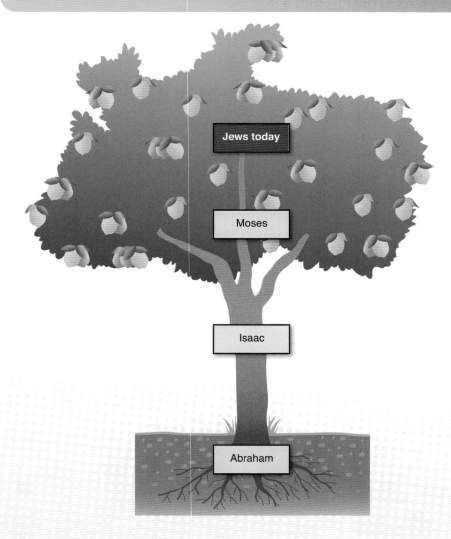

Jews today

Moses

Isaac

Abraham

Judaism is passed down through the family: for Orthodox Jews a person is Jewish if their mother is Jewish. Many Progressive Jews will say that a person is Jewish if either one of their parents is Jewish. What would happen to the Jewish religion if there were no Jewish families?

Judaism is a religion that is passed down through families and it focuses most of its religious practices and customs in the home. Often in Judaism children have a unique part to play in religious celebrations, for example during the Feast of Lights, named **Hanukkah**, Jewish children play a special game with a spinning top called a dreidel. This game helps the children to remember part of the history of the event that they are celebrating.

In Judaism each person in the family has responsibilities. Children have responsibilities to their parents and parents have responsibilities to their children. In this sense everyone contributes to the family and to Jewish society.

What benefits do you think there are to a religion of incorporating games into festival celebrations?

Knowledge check

1 Who is the father of Judaism?

2 What determines whether a person is Jewish?

3 Where are most customs and traditions in Judaism celebrated or remembered?

4 In what way are children and parents alike in Judaism?

The Jewish father must

... support his family.

... study the Torah.

... make sure his children study the Torah.

The Jewish mother must

... provide the family with kosher food.

... make sure the husband and children have the right clothes.

... prepare the home for the Shabbat and the festivals.

... teach her daughters what they need to know when they grow up.

The Jewish children must

... respect their mother and father.

... look after their parents as they become elderly.

... listen to their father.

... make their parents proud.

Marriage in Judaism is a commitment that is meant to be made for life. The husband has promised to look after his wife, and if they have any he has promised to care for his children. Divorce is not desirable but sometimes it may be necessary, even in a Jewish marriage. A possible reason a Jew may want a divorce would be if their spouse had an affair, this is known as adultery and it is forbidden in the Torah.

If a couple decide to divorce the husband must give his wife a get, this is a divorce document from a Bet Din. This is what is commanded as the correct practice in the Torah. The divorce can then only take place after three months to check that the wife is not pregnant. Without a get neither the man or the woman can remarry. Progressive Jews now allow women to obtain a get.

Activity A

1 Using the title 'A Guide to Jewish Family Life', create a leaflet that explains the responsibilities of parents and children within a Jewish family.

2 Use the information on this page to help you.

3 Find out more about each role through further research.

Activity B

1 Design a questionnaire to find out what responsibilities your peers have in their own families.

2 Gather your results. You may use diagrams or graphs to help you to do this.

3 Compare the results of your questionnaire to what you know about children's responsibilities in Jewish families. What conclusions do you come to?

Activity C

1 In small groups discuss whether it is helpful for there to be clearly defined roles within a family.

2 Record your discussion by writing each point on a separate index card.

3 Next arrange the cards in an order that you think would create an interesting discussion.

4 Each person in the group now needs to write up the group's discussion following the order that your group chose to put the cards in.

5 When writing up the discussion you should try to link the end of one paragraph to the start of the next one.

6 At the end of your write up provide a personal summary that explains whether you believe it to be helpful for there to be clearly defined roles in a family.

Activity D

'It is unreasonable to expect a couple to commit themselves to one another until they die.'

1 Do you agree with this statement?

2 What responses might a Jew offer?

3.4 What was the Holocaust?

Learning objectives

You will ...
- know what the Holocaust was
- understand some of the effects of the Holocaust on the Jewish people
- identify strategies through which events like the Holocaust can be prevented in the future
- evaluate the human ability to forgive.

The **Holocaust** was the killing of approximately 6 million Jews before and during the Second World War. The Jews often refer to the Holocaust as 'Shoah', which is Hebrew for catastrophe.

From 1933 until the end of the Second World War the Nazis ruled Germany, led by Adolf Hitler. Hitler believed that the Jewish people were inferior to other human beings. He made it his goal to kill every Jew in Europe. As Hitler gained more and more ground across Europe he steadily developed his plan and created a terrible mechanism for the mass killing of Jews. Hitler's army rounded up Jews across Europe and took them to **concentration camps** where they were separated from all their possessions and their families.

The Jews did not have their own land at this time; they were a people scattered throughout Europe and the world. This made it hard for the Jews to unite together and to resist the evil of Hitler.

Many Jews were forced to work in awful conditions and with little food, and this alone led to thousands of deaths. Other Jews were sent straight to their deaths in chambers that housed 2000 people at a time. The chambers were filled with gas and the people inside died. Hitler ordered the killing of more than 6 million Jews and other minority groups during this terrible period in history.

Jews were taken from their homes and put in concentration camps. Their lives were destroyed by the Nazi army.

Knowledge check

Read pages 60–61.

1 What happened during the Holocaust?
2 Who was the Nazi leader?
3 What did the Nazi leader believe about the Jews?
4 When do Jews believe that it is acceptable to use violence?

For many Jews this time in their history reinforces their teaching that at times violence in war must be used to stand up against evil. The Jewish philosopher Martin Buber once said that he did not want to need to use force, but if that was required to beat evil then he would use it, and he would trust God's judgement of him.

When speaking of these atrocities Rabbi Albert Friedlander said:

'… an act of forgiveness is a relationship between humans requiring action from both sides. But you cannot go to the 6 million. They are dead; I cannot speak for them. Nor can I speak for God.'

A Holocaust memorial to commemorate those who lost their lives. This one is in Miami, Florida.

Activity A

Using the information in this chapter create a newspaper front page that describes what the Holocaust was.

Activity B

There are many memorials dedicated to those who were killed during the Holocaust.

1 Find out more about what happened to the Jews during the Holocaust.

2 Design a memorial that would help people commemorate those who lost their lives.

3 Provide a written explanation for the final design that you produce.

Activity C

At Dachau concentration camp, which is now a museum, the phrase 'Never Again' is written on the wall.

1 In small groups discuss why it is important to learn about the events of the Holocaust.

2 Use a spidergram to generate ideas about how an event like the Holocaust could be avoided in the future.

3 Present your ideas in a class discussion. Through the discussion identify the idea that you believe to be the best.

Activity D

Read the quotation above from Rabbi Albert Friedlander.

1 Explain what you think the rabbi means when he says 'an act of forgiveness is a relationship between humans requiring action from both sides'.

2 Do you agree with this idea? Give reasons for your answer.

3 Do you think there could ever be forgiveness for the Holocaust? Use the quotation and the information in this chapter to help you.

3.5 What do Jews believe about war and peace?

Learning objectives

You will ...
- understand Jewish attitudes towards war and peace
- find out about the Arab-Israeli conflict
- evaluate the human ability to forgive.

Jews believe that the world will one day be a place of peace. Isaiah, a **prophet** of the Jewish Bible, predicted a time when weapons will no longer be needed – they will be turned into tools. The Hebrew word for peace is 'Shalom'. Jews use it as a greeting.

That time hasn't come yet. The Torah teaches that, when there is conflict, Jews should try to make peace. But that isn't always possible. Jews believe that war is sometimes necessary, so they are not **pacifists**.

The Torah describes battles the Israelites fought because God ordered them to. Jews believe there are also times when they need to use force to defend themselves. In Judaism there are two main types of war that must be fought (see right).

Milchemet Mitzvah

- A war commanded by God.
- For example, God told Joshua, an Israelite leader, to fight for land on several occasions; each time God gave him victory.
- The enemy must either be about to attack OR has attacked.

Milchemet Reshut

- An optional war.
- It is used to defend a country and to prevent war from spreading.
- This should be the last option after all else has been tried.
- Damage must be limited.
- Civilians must not be targeted.

Knowledge check

Read pages 62–63.

1 What is a prophet?
2 What did the prophet Isaiah foretell about the future?
3 How does the traditional Jewish greeting reflect that Jews are a peaceful people?
4 Are Jews pacifists? How do you know this?
5 What are the two types of war in Judaism that are believed to be necessary and acceptable?
6 What is the cause of conflict in Israel?
7 Who currently occupies Gaza and the West Bank?
8 How do the Israelis believe the conflict has to be resolved?

Activity A

Create a poster promoting peace. Include:

a the word 'Shalom'

b a prophetic quotation from either Isaiah 2:4 or Micah 4:4

c images that reflect Jewish teaching on peace.

An ongoing source of conflict exists between the Jews and Palestinians in the State of Israel.

After the Jews were given the State of Israel in 1948 there was a great deal of conflict between the Israelis and the Palestinians. In 1964 the Palestine Liberation Organization (PLO) was founded. The main belief held by the PLO was that Palestine was the land of the Arab Palestinian people. Israel did not accept the PLO as a group that they needed to negotiate with. Eventually in 1988, Yasser Arafat, the Palestinian leader at that time, said that he accepted Israel's right to exist. Following this in 1993 there was an attempt to create two separate states, a Palestinian and an Israeli State. This was called the Oslo Peace Process. This allowed the PLO to run two areas in Israel called the Gaza Strip and the West Bank. However an important part of this process was that the Palestinians were expected to recognise the equal existence of the State of Israel and terrorist activities by the Palestinians had to stop.

Fatah is one Palestinian political party, and it says it is willing to exist alongside Israel providing Palestinians are given more political rights. Another main Palestinian political group is Hamas. Hamas does not recognise the State of Israel.

Almost half a million Israelis live in more than 200 settlements in the West Bank and East Jerusalem. In September 2011 the Israelis announced the building of a further 1100 homes to expand their settlement in Gilo which is on the outskirts of Jerusalem. These settlements are illegal according to international law, although Israel disagrees with this.

In 2010 the Palestinians asked individual countries to recognise Palestine as an independent state in order to be accepted into the United Nations. The Palestinians claim that this would help with peace talks with Israel. Fatah back this plan. Israel however believe that peace is needed through negotiation not through the Palestinians being accepted into the UN.

Activity C

1 Work in small groups. Discuss the circumstances you believe are acceptable to cause a country to go to war. Write these down as a list.

2 Using the circumstances that you have listed as a guide, discuss what makes Hitler's attack (see pages 60–61) on the Jews unacceptable.

3 Share your solutions with the class.

Activity B

1 In pairs find out more about Joshua's call to Milchemet Mitzvah by reading Joshua chapter 8.

2 Imagine you are a news reporter in the region at that time. In your pair create a radio interview with Joshua after the battle for Ai has been won.

3 Think about the questions you could ask Joshua about why he fought the battle.

4 Create the kind of answers that you think Joshua may have given.

5 Write this up as a script and record your interview.

Activity D

Both the Israelis and the Palestinians believe that they have a claim to the land of Israel. They have both been aggressive towards one another and people have lost their lives in this dispute.

1 Investigate more about the current conflict between the Israelis and the Palestinians.

2 In small groups consider what each group wants.

3 In your group decide what you think the next step towards peace should be for the Palestinians and the Israelis.

4 Discuss why you think this is not happening and what could be done to overcome this.

5 Write a letter to the United Nations outlining the conclusions from your group work.

3.6 What do Jews believe about issues of life and death?

Learning objectives

You will ...
- learn what abortion and euthanasia are
- understand the moral questions surrounding these issues
- evaluate Jewish attitudes towards at least one of these issues.

Judaism teaches that humans were created by God. God is believed to be the one who chooses when each person lives and when they die. In this sense Jews believe that God has a plan for each person's life. In certain situations, such as Milchemet Mitzvah, killing is believed to be acceptable but taking human life is not generally considered right. This is because of the statement in Exodus 20, which states that people should not murder.

Abortion

Abortion is a medical act that causes the foetus to leave the woman's womb, and which leads to its death. There has been much discussion in Judaism over when human life actually begins. This affects Jewish beliefs about abortion. In the **Mishnah** it suggests that it is only at birth that the foetus becomes a life as valuable as that of the mother. Before birth Jews consider the mother's life to be the most important. Many Jews therefore accept that there are certain circumstances in which abortion is acceptable, for example, if the pregnancy is endangering the mother's life or if the child will be born with severe disabilities.

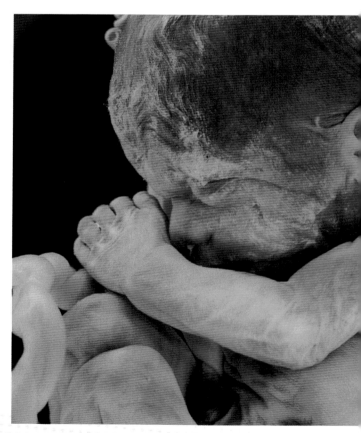

This is a foetus at twelve weeks. When do you think human life begins?

Euthanasia

Euthanasia comes from two Greek words which mean 'good death'. It is used to refer to situations when people are helped to die. Often people want this because they have a terminal illness or a severe disability.

Jews do not accept that it is right to end life even when a person is facing difficult and challenging medical situations. They believe that as a person lives, God works through their experiences and circumstances. This means that even through illness God is working in a person's life, so for this reason Jews reject euthanasia.

Jews believe that God is the only one with the authority to decide when a person should die. Some Jews do accept the turning off of life-support machines, which is a form of euthanasia, because it allows nature to take its course – if God chooses, the person will die. Jews believe that doctors have a responsibility to save life but not to prolong it beyond what God may intend.

Knowledge check

1 Who do Jews believe has a plan for everyone's life?

2 When a woman is pregnant whose life is considered most important in Judaism, her life or the life of the unborn child?

3 How does this belief affect the Jewish view on abortion?

4 In Judaism why is suffering not considered a reason to allow someone to seek euthanasia?

5 Why do many Jews believe turning off a life-support machine is an acceptable thing to do?

Activity A

1 Create an advert that promotes Jewish teaching on either abortion or euthanasia.

2 Your advert could be for TV, radio or for use on a billboard.

Activity B

1 In small groups discuss the reasons for and against supporting either abortion or euthanasia.

2 Does your group agree or disagree with the Jewish teaching?

3 Record your discussion in the form of a see-saw diagram.

4 Below your completed diagram provide a written explanation for the outcome of your discussion.

Activity C

1 In small groups write three or more letters to a problem page in a magazine. Each letter should be asking for guidance on either abortion or euthanasia.

2 Once the letters are complete discuss in your group the Jewish responses that you would expect to each of the problems.

3 Next, each person in the group should be allocated one letter to write a Jewish response to.

4 Once complete arrange the letters and their replies to create the final problem page for a magazine.

Activity D

In Judaism killing is generally unacceptable. Shedding blood is another phrase that may be used to mean killing. In the **Talmud** it says, 'He who closes the eyes of a dying man while the soul is still departing is shedding blood. This may be compared to a lamp that is going out; if a man places his finger upon it, it is immediately extinguished.'

1 Explain what you think this teaching means.

2 Do you agree with the teaching? Give reasons for your answer.

3 Describe and then explain why someone may hold an opposite view to your own.

3.7 What do Jews believe about wealth and poverty?

Learning objectives

You will ...
- find out what Judaism teaches about money
- understand how Jews give to charity
- evaluate Jewish teachings on wealth and poverty.

'The best way of giving is to help a person help themselves so that they may become self-supporting.'
(Maimonides, a Jewish thinker)

'There will always be poor people in the land. Therefore I command you to be open handed toward your fellow Israelites who are poor and needy in your land.'
(Deuteronomy 15:11)

As you can see from the above quotations, Jews believe that generosity towards those in need is a duty for them all. Jews believe that God decides who is rich and who is poor; neither situation is wrong. However, if a wealthy person becomes obsessed with money and possessions and neglects those less well off then this is wrong.

As the quotation from Deuteronomy makes clear, those who have money are required to give to those who are poor, but not to the extent that they then become poor themselves.

This is a **pushke**. What questions could you ask a Jew to discover more about what it is and why Jews would use it?

Knowledge check

Read pages 66–67.

1 What do Jews think about being wealthy?
2 Why is being obsessed with money considered wrong in Judaism?
3 What percentage of their wealth do Jews aim to give to charity?
4 What are pushkes?
5 How is gemilat chassadim different to tzedakah?

Tzedakah

All Jews are expected to give a tenth of their wealth as **tzedekah**. Tzedakah is the Hebrew word for the acts that we call charity in English: giving aid, help and money to the poor and needy. In Judaism, giving to the poor is not viewed as a generous act. It is simply an act of justice and righteousness.

In their homes Jews have pushkes. These are collection boxes and Jews, including the children, use them to give part of their money to charity.

When Jews seek to give to the poor they do so to try to help those in **poverty** to become self-supporting again. The Jewish thinker Maimonides said this was the best form of giving.

Gemilat chassadim

Another type of giving in Judaism is **gemilat chassadim**. This form of giving means to carry out a kind action. This type of care for the needy may include soup kitchens for homeless people, helping an elderly person in their home or even offering a kind and encouraging word to someone.

Judaism and the world of work

While all Jews believe that it is God who decides a person's wealth they also believe that every person has the responsibility to work.

The Torah makes it clear to the Jewish people that while they must work they must also make time to study the Torah and obey God's commands.

Most importantly, Jews must observe the Sabbath. On the Sabbath Jews must not work. However, work that saves lives on the Sabbath is allowed.

Any work a Jew does must also be honest and any products they sell must be of good quality.

Activity A

1 Design and make a pushke box.
2 On the outside of the box add text and pictures to remind the user why giving in this way is important in Judaism.

Activity B

Deuteronomy 15:11 tells Jews that they must be open handed to the poor and needy.

1 Design an advert to recruit Jews as volunteers in a charity organisation of your choice.
2 In your advert make links to the quotations from Deuteronomy and Maimonides on page 66.
3 Make sure you give reasons to encourage Jews to apply to be volunteers in your advert.

Activity C

1 In small groups discuss what a poor Jewish person may do for charity. Record your ideas in a list.
2 Discuss in your group whether you think it is important that the poor can contribute to acts of charity. What reasons can your group come up with?
3 Use a spidergram to record your ideas.
4 Summarise your group work by writing a paragraph about each of the areas that you discussed. Remember to give reasons to support the points that you make.

Activity D

1 Do you agree that what people do to make money is important or is it just important to make money?
2 Write a careers pamphlet with appropriate/suitable jobs for Jews.

The big assignment

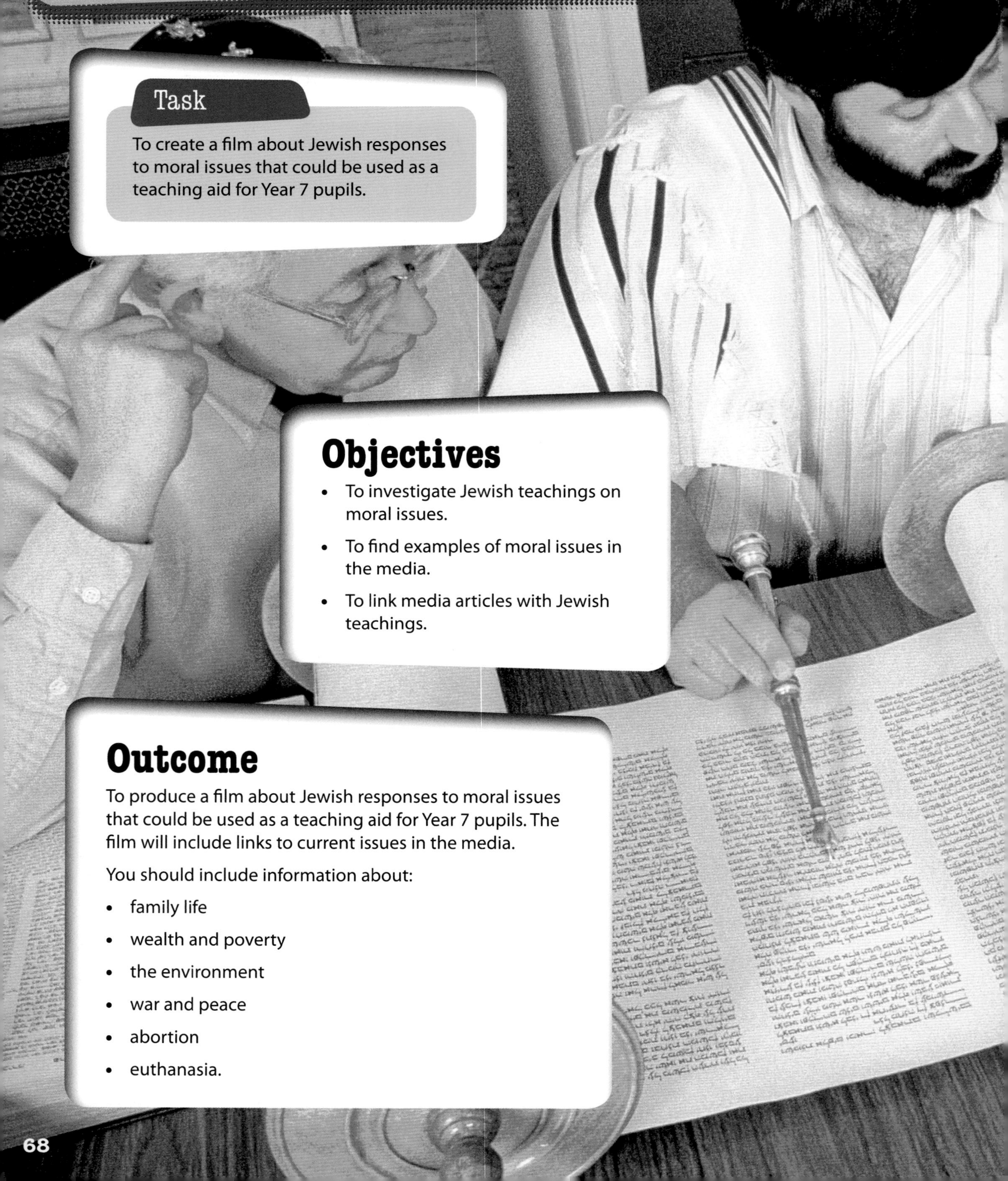

Task

To create a film about Jewish responses to moral issues that could be used as a teaching aid for Year 7 pupils.

Objectives

- To investigate Jewish teachings on moral issues.
- To find examples of moral issues in the media.
- To link media articles with Jewish teachings.

Outcome

To produce a film about Jewish responses to moral issues that could be used as a teaching aid for Year 7 pupils. The film will include links to current issues in the media.

You should include information about:

- family life
- wealth and poverty
- the environment
- war and peace
- abortion
- euthanasia.

Guidance

1 Work in groups of six people. Each person should be given a particular moral issue to investigate.

2 Pupils who are Jewish should act as advisors to the group.

3 For each issue research what the Torah teaches.

4 Find at least one reasonably current news story about your issue.

5 Make notes on how Jews may respond to the story/stories. If possible interview a local rabbi or members of the Jewish community and gather their views on the story/stories.

6 As a group decide on the style that each section of your film will take. Identify the strengths of the individuals in your group as you plan the production of your film. You may consider one or more of the following possible formats for your film:

   a An interview-style presentation in which one or more of your group takes on the role of a Jewish person as the interview is filmed.
   b An animated section of film, for example using Flash software.
   c A combination of video, text and animation, for example using Movie Maker software.
   d A filmed role play with commentary added at the end or during the scenes.

7 As a group complete the preparation of the six sections of your film.

8 Your completed film should comprise six sections that can be watched all the way through or that could be shown to a class one section at a time.

9 Ask a Year 7 tutor if they would show your film to their tutor group. You could also ask the rabbi of the local synagogue to watch your film. Ask them for feedback.

10 As a group, evaluate your film. Decide what you did well and what you could have done to improve it.

Assessment

You will be assessed on:

✓ how well you use specialist vocabulary

✓ the accuracy of your accounts of Jewish teachings

✓ your ability to explain how the teachings apply to real-life situations.

Glossary

Abortion Removal of the foetus from the womb before it can survive.

Abraham Founder of the Jewish religion.

Adonai Name given to God which means Lord.

Ark Cupboard in the synagogue where the Torah scrolls are kept.

Bar Mitzvah Meaning 'Son of the Commandment'. Celebrating a boy becoming responsible for his religious duties.

Bat Mitzvah Meaning 'Daughter of the Commandment'. Celebrating a girl becoming responsible for her religious duties

Bimah Platform on which the reading desk stands in the synagogue.

Brit Milah Circumcision ceremony of baby boys, eight days after their birth.

Challah Bread used particularly on Shabbat and during festivals.

Chazan Leader in an Orthodox service; he chants the prayers and sings.

Circumcision A small operation to remove the flap of skin at the end of the penis.

Concentration camps Camps where Jews were imprisoned by the Nazis.

Covenant Solemn agreement or promise.

Diaspora Scattering of Jews across the Middle East and throughout Europe.

Eternal Lasting forever.

Euthanasia The painless killing of someone dying from a terminal illness.

Gemilat chassadim A form of giving in Judaism that involves acting in a way to help others.

Hagadah A booklet that describes the order for celebrating the Pesach meal.

Halakhic A life walking with God, obeying him.

Hanukkah A winter festival that remembers how Judah the Maccabee obeyed God and helped the Jews to capture Jerusalem.

Havdalah A prayer said on Saturday sunset at the end of Shabbat.

Idols Things worshipped in the place of God, such as statues.

Jerusalem The holy city for Jews.

Kaddish A Jewish prayer recited by mourners.

Kiddush A blessing said at the beginning of the Sabbath.

Kippah A prayer cap.

Kosher Permitted; food that is allowed.

Mantle Covering placed over the Torah scrolls when they are not in use.

Messiah The hoped for saviour of the Jews.

Midrash Collections of commentaries from rabbis on the Tenakh.

Mishnah The first section of the Tal mud, or the teaching of a rabbi on Jewish laws.

Mitzvah (pl. Mitzvot) Commandment.

Mohel A Jewish man trained in circumcision.

Monotheism (monotheistic) Religious belief in only one God.

Ner tamid Lamp that hangs above the Ark in the synagogue and never goes out.

Olam Ha-Ba This is the life to come after death.

Orthodox Jew 'Traditional' Jew.

Pacifists People who refuse to use any form of violence.

Pesach The Passover festival that remembers how God rescued the Jews from slavery in Egypt.

Polytheism Religious belief in many gods.

Poverty A lack or shortage of money.

Prophet Someone who tells people God's messages.

Purim A festival that celebrates the rescue of the Jews from destruction.

Pushke A small money box used to save money for charity.

Rabbi Teacher, especially in the synagogue.

Reformed Jew More 'modern' Jew.

Rite of passage A ritual that celebrates significant moments in life.

Rosh Hashanah Jewish New Year festival.

Sabbath Jewish day of rest and worship to God. Beginning Friday sunset and ending on sunset Saturday.

Sedar Family meal on the first night of Pesach.

Shabbat Jewish day of rest and worship.

Shavuot A Jewish festival celebrating God giving the Ten Statements to Moses as well as thanks for the harvest.

Shema The most important Jewish prayer.

Shiva Seven days of mourning beginning on the day of a funeral.

Shofar A form of trumpet made from a ram's horn.

Shroud Cloth used to wrap a dead body in preparation for burial.

Siddur Jewish prayer book.

Sofar A Jewish scribe who handwrites the Torah.

Star of David The symbol of Judaism.

Stewardship Care for the world and all created things.

Sukkot Feast of Tabernacles, a Jewish festival.

Synagogue Jewish place of meeting and worship.

Tallit Prayer shawl.

Talmud Collected teachings of the Rabbis.

Tenakh the 24 books that make up the Jewish scriptures.

Torah Five books of Jewish law.

Tzedekah An act of charity.

Yad A pointer, often made from silver, used to follow the words in the Torah.

Yahrzeit Anniversary of a death.

Yom Kippur Day of Atonement. It is a fast day that happens ten days after Rosh Hashanah.

Index